357/45

Falkirk Council

Feeding Scotland

Catherine Brown

N·M·S

NATIONAL MUSEUMS OF SCOTLAND

Published by the National Museums of Scotland
Chambers Street, Edinburgh EH1 1JF

ISBN 0 948636 84 X

© Catherine Brown and the Trustees of the National
Museums of Scotland 1996

British Library Cataloguing in Publication Data
A catalogue record for this book is available from the
British Library

The author asserts her moral right to be identified as the author of this work
and the publishers undertake to observe such assertion and impose the same
condition on its licensees.

Series editor Iseabail Macleod

Designed and produced by the Publications Office of
the National Museums of Scotland

Printed in Great Britain on Huntsman Velvet 110g²m
by Clifford Press Ltd, Coventry

＊

Acknowledgements

We are grateful to the National Museums of Scotland Charitable Trust for
support for this publication.

Illustrations: Front cover: National Gallery of Scotland. Back cover: Courtesy
Tom McIlwraith. 4: Western Isles Island Council. 6, 12, 15, 16, 20, 22, 25,
29, 33, 37, ii, vi, vii top and bottom, viii top and bottom, 42, 44, 45, 46, 49, 50,
59, 60, 66, 67, 69, 75, 78: NMS. 8 top and bottom: The Mellerstain Trust.
31: School of Scottish Studies. 32: G W Dey. 35: Nairn Fishertown Museum.
40: Neil Short. i: Historic Scotland. iii top and bottom: Trustees of the
National Library of Scotland. iv, v: National Trust for Scotland. 45: Molly
Skeene. 53: The Mitchell Library, Glasgow. 57: Norman Chalmers. 62: Dr
Bruce Walker. 65: The Iain Thornber Collection. 74: Biggar Museums
Trust.

Front cover: *Detail from* The Penny Wedding *by David
Allan 1795.*

Back cover: *Detail from* The Hairst Rig, *an illustration from*
Life and Works of Robert Burns *by P Hately Waddell*

CONTENTS

INTRODUCTION

It might be imagined that the early Scots, with their pastoral system of agriculture, would have been predominantly meat-eaters. Yet although meat was eaten throughout most of Scotland, animals were regarded first and foremost as a source of income or draught. They were used for producing milk, butter and cheese, and were sold on the hoof, primarily in exchange for other necessities.

A more important source of protein foods came from Scotland's extensive coastal waters. They provided a rich source of fish and shellfish and a strong fishing tradition developed around the coastline, with many lively fishing communities, particularly on the east coast and the islands. Another factor which encouraged fish-eating was the influence of the monasteries during the medieval period, when compulsory fish days meant that for large parts of the year people were obliged to survive on an entirely meat-free diet.

Apart from short periods in spring and summer, both meat and fish were eaten salted, dried and smoked, so methods of cooking had to be adapted to dealing with these highly piquant foods. Eventually, in the eighteenth century, it was discovered how to 'winter' animals on root vegetables, and salting, drying and smoking became less necessary. A whole range of less well-preserved foods with a shorter shelf-life, such as the kipper, was developed.

Before the first Scottish recipes appear, early in the eighteenth century, information about Scotland's diet can be found in

Cod, halibut and ling laid out on the quay at Stornoway, Lewis, in about 1906. The scene suggests an abundance of food from the sea, a vital part of the Scottish diet. SEA

Salt has always been a key to the preservation and flavour of food in Scotland. 'Toby' salt cellars were popular in the nineteenth century, many of them made in Prestonpans.

records of trade, agriculture and fishing, as well as from descriptions by travellers and locals. Household account books of lairds and their families are also a rich source of detail about food and eating for both masters and servants. The food and drink of the rich were enlivened by trade, and there is evidence that spices were imported from southern Europe and beyond, from very early times. From the Middle Ages, trade with Europe grew, with particular influence from Scotland's long connections with France.

There was a huge gap between the luxurious food of the rich and the daily fare of the poor. The land-owning classes not only ate much more protein than their tenants, they also drank differently, consuming staggering amounts of imported wine, especially claret, while the lower classes drank ale and whisky made from local grains.

Because of its northern situation Scotland has never been a great grain-producing country. Wheat has only been grown in quantity in the exceptionally favoured Lothians. The main cereal crops have been oats and a particularly hardy form of barley known as bere or bear, still grown in Orkney. The Highlands and the Southern Uplands were seldom self-sufficient in grain and a pattern developed of exchange of grain and protein between these areas and the central Lowlands. But the largest trade was in cattle from the Highlands, driven south to markets such as Crieff and Falkirk, to be exchanged for lowland grain and other produce.

Disaster might strike in the form of crop failure and up until the eighteenth century widespread famine occurred two or three times a century. But outside these exceptional years the evidence suggests that Scottish diets were adequate.

The discovery of the New World revolutionized the diet, bringing many new foods and in particular the potato. Like all novel foods, it was initially a luxury available only to the wealthy, taking many years to become part of the daily diet. But during the late eighteenth and nineteenth centuries it became the staple food of the Highlands. In the cities, although there was easier access to imported foods, the diet of the urban poor was much less nutritious than the traditional rural diet.

The changes and improvements in food production of the eighteenth and nineteenth centuries took much longer to reach the remoter and poorer parts of the Highlands and Islands, where the old ways continued until comparatively recently. In these areas, imported foods and brick ovens remained completely unknown. Not for them the subtleties of exotic spicing or the soft springiness of a freshly-baked yeasted loaf. Beef was boiled in its hide and unplucked game birds wrapped in clay and roasted in the embers. Meal and water were mixed to a stiff paste and cooked in a thin pancake on a hot stone, in a tradition going back to prehistoric times.

Those who have an interest in Scotland's cooking past - in action - may wish to attempt some of the dishes cooked in a different age, capturing some of the authenticity of contemporary eating habits. A few recipes have been included, and there is also a list (see page 79) of suggested sources of historical recipes.

Mellerstaine Janry 1714 Expence Houghold Furniture

For a Dozen of knives & forks .... 7.
For 16 before mutchken botles 1 2 8
For 3 plain hearth brooms 1 3
For 13 lame Delph plates 8
To McKenzie Gold smith for workmanship of the silver Coffie pot & Milk pot at 20 p ounce & there was some ods in the weight of plate I gave him to make them off they weight 56 ounces 14 drop and three handles cost 17 .... 6 8 3
To Dicon orcheltry for winding at the spinel & warping ale for betwixt 5 & 6 ship yenn & for puting on the name 3 11
For 2 backeing pots 16, 4 Brown porangers 6, a mutchken Juge for heating ale 2, a chesing 2 4

Lady Grisell Baillie presided over Mellerstain House, Berwickshire, in the early eighteenth century. Like the account books of the Foulis family, her household books provide a fascinating insight into food and meals.

8

FEEDING SCOTLAND

1 A pastoral cooking, brightly influenced by France

On a country estate of rolling farmlands to the north-east of Corstorphine Hill the seventeenth-century laird of Ravelston, John Foulis, and his family enjoyed a life of plentiful and varied food and fine wines. While he farmed his land, and sold surplus produce in the city markets, he also kept details of the family's household expenditure in a leather-bound book, adding notes among the income and expenditure: some bricks had fallen out of the bread oven... a new kitchen chimney had been built... he was off to an Edinburgh tavern for an oyster supper... to Leith for a game of golf... to the river Cramond to fish...

As Foulis wrote, the capital was still surrounded by a medieval wall with a twenty-four hour guard. Yet the contents of the Foulis larder and cellar illustrate the sophisticated lifestyle of a modestly well-off laird with a liking for fine wines and spirits. He paid many visits to his wine merchant in Leith, jaunted to Edinburgh for a night of gambling in the city taverns, bought sweetmeats for his wife and chestnuts and gingerbread for his children.

His household books reveal an eating pattern which exploited every available resource from land and sea in the local vicinity. Yet the people were not entirely self-sufficient. Spices and citrus fruits, for instance, were certainly not produced in Scotland. Cheeses came from Ireland. But the most substantial import to the Ravelston diet was the mature claret and fine brandy from France which cost Foulis more in a year than the combined cost of maintaining his house and farm. His cook, he says, was called Marie.

For her daily cooking she had, according to the seasons, parsnips, leeks, turnips, asparagus, carrots, salad vegetables, parsley and syboes. Apples, pears, plums and apricots came from the orchard. From the winter food-stores, besides the pickles and preserves which were made at the end of the summer, she had preserved hams, Irish cheeses, barrels of salt herring, pickled oysters, dried fish, solan geese (gannets) and anchovies.

There was a permanent supply of loaf sugar, butter, salad oil, vinegar and salt; occasionally dried figs, prunes, raisins, nuts, aniseed, chestnuts, lemons, oranges, pomegranates, cinnamon, mustard seed, cumin, cardamoms and fenugreek, were used. She used very little tea, coffee or chocolate which were only bought rarely and in very small quantities. Wheat bread was very expensive and was bought only from time to time from an Edinburgh baker. The home farm provided grain, mostly barley and oats, also beef and lamb, while tenants paid their rent in kind (*kain*) with chickens and grain.

Her cooking equipment consisted of a three-gallon iron pot over an open fire, a flat metal plate, which also hung over the open fire where she 'girdle-baked'. The brick-lined oven was heated with wood faggots for bread-baking and an open spit was used for roasting in front of the fire.

Though the first Scottish cookery book was not published until 1736, a manuscript collection of recipes by Martha Brown of Ayrshire (1710) reveals the kind of dishes which might have been popular around the time Foulis was keeping his books. Yet another manuscript written by Lady Castlehill of Cambusnethan (1712), consisting of some 400 handwritten recipes bound in leather, are another source of information, shedding more light on Scotland's early feeding.

All of this makes it clear that one of the central eating traditons was the system of making a pot of *strong broth*. It was the cook's task each day to manage her day round this focal point of the daily feeding, a process which can be reconstructed, as it might have taken place in the Ravelston family kitchen in about 1690.

Work began at daybreak as Marie hitched the handle of the muckle black pot onto a hook over the open coal fire in the basket grate, the smoke catching her throat and watering her eyes. Until a new chimney was built, blow-downs plagued the kitchen, covering it with soot when the wind blew in the wrong direction. She filled the pot almost full with three gallons of cold water which had been carried from the well in a wooden luggie, and it heated up slowly.

A wide baronial archway separated fire and pot from the main kitchen, where she went to cut the meat from a leg of fresh beef. Large chunks of beef, the bones, three onions stuck with a dozen cloves and a bundle of sweet herbs went into the pot. There was a lid for protection from soot drips coming down the chimney. By the time the family sat down to their morning brose at eight, this first part of her broth-making procedure was almost completed.

Throughout this cooking, she attended to the fire so that the broth cooked 'softly' with a gentle heat. Broth-making became an instinctive part of her cooking life, the basis for the family's every-day food, success a long, careful simmer over a slow fire. By the middle of the morning the onions would be in a mush, the beef tender and the liquid rich and concentrated with many flavours.

She strained it, lifted out the beef and put it onto a cold marble shelf in the larder. Onions and herbs had done their task of flavouring and went out. Bones were either given to animals or kept for beggars at the back door. The highly flavoured, strained liquid (stock) known as 'strong broth' was ready for future use.

Once this had been prepared, for the second stage soaked barley or peas were added to lithe (thicken) the broth. Some fresh vegetables, which had been finely chopped, were also added, plus fresh herbs and a few scraggy kain hens, which had been handed into the kitchen from the laird's tenants. There were a few finishing touches, such as handfuls of fresh young sorrel leaves, before the well-seasoned and aromatic liquid was poured into an immense 'charger' and carried by one of the man servants through to the laird's dining table and placed before him, to be served to family and servants.

The finished aromatic broth might have joined on the table: an ashet of cold beef, a kebbuck (whole cheese) from their own farm, a stone jar of freshly churned butter, baskets of soft bannocks, a bowl of ripe plums from the house orchard and a heap of oysters from the Forth piled up on a wooden board. While pewter broth-trenchers were set round the table at everyone's place, Sir John presided in his high-backed chair at one end with his family around him, indoor servants at the other end. Everyone was served a share of the ambrosial liquid along with a morsel of hen and a slice of beef. The servants drank home-brewed ale while the family and children drank claret from a pewter stoup (flagon) taken from a hogshead (barrel) in the cellar. It was the main hot meal of the day.

While it might seem an unusual sophistication to make a basic stock first, this method (also firmly rooted in French cuisine)

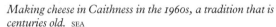

Making cheese in Caithness in the 1960s, a tradition that is centuries old. SEA

became an instinctive part of the Scottish broth-making tradition and probably developed its style from the ties between Scotland and France going back to the thirteenth century. The Scots language by this time had absorbed words such as 'gigot' and 'ashet' and it seems likely that the Scots also picked up their refined broth-making techniques from their ancient French connection. Certainly, according to these early recipes, they copied the French system of starting first with a *pot au feu* or stock pot, using the highly flavourful liquid as a basis for future development. Employing the stock system formed the basis of a repertoire of many original and notable Scottish broths which have become classic examples of making the most of indigenous raw materials in an aromatic and sustaining brew appropriate to the climate and the needs of the people.

2 The rich Highland larder

In the Highlands a more hazardous lifestyle was in contrast to the comfortable life of a Lowland laird. The people not only lived in a very different environment, they also spoke a different language, and depended for their sources of food supply on entirely different raw materials, creating separate eating traditions.

In 1715 the twenty-second chief of the clan MacDougall, Iain Ciar (dark John) lived in a six-foot thick walled tower fortress on the edge of a sea cliff overlooking the northern entrance to Oban Bay. He made no detailed household recordings of day-to-day expenditures, but he did write letters and the castle contents were noted in inventories recorded each time a clan chief died. Unlike Ravelston House, which no longer exists, the ruins of Dunollie Castle still stand. A stair from the cellars leads up to the old hall where there are two fire hearths on opposite walls, one for people to congregate round for warmth, the other for cooking.

According to the inventories, the cook's equipment consisted of a large cauldron, two big and two small 'potts'; two small copper skillets; two brass pans; a frying pan; an old girdle; a brander (grill); three pairs of tongs; a ladle; a strainer; and a grater. In the fireplace there was a roasting rack and three long spits which rested on hooks above the stone arch when not in use. In addition there were shelved stone recesses, still visible, in the walls to store everyday essentials like salt and meal. The rest of the hall, it appears from the inventory details, was not lavishly furnished, but there were the essentials for comfort. The carved wooden trestle table had a linen cloth. There was some fine delft-ware and silver, pewter plates, wooden bowls, horn spoons, a dealing spoon (or serving spoon), a salt dish and a mustard dish.

For a breakfast in the castle (about 1715) the morning's work might have started with cattle-milking. A supply of water was brought in from the burn, while the nooks and crannies of out-buildings and courtyard would have to be searched for newly laid hens eggs. Meanwhile the cook would have started the fire and the pot of mealy porridge would have been heaving and bubbling for several hours before people congregated in the hall for their first hot meal of the day, which lasted them through until evening.

Their habit was to stand round the communal porridge pot, supping with their horn spoons, dipping the hot spoonfuls into a bowl of thick fresh cream, making the contrast of hot porridge and cold cream which is both warming and satisfying. To follow there would be freshly boiled eggs to crack and eat with a soft bannock and a slice of soft goat's milk cheese, and to drink ale and butter-milk, or for those whose meal was not complete without a swig of potent whisky, a stone bottle of *usquebae* sat on the table.

This everyday breakfast might have been augmented with other delicacies such as cold roasts, fried fish, pickled meats and fruit pre-serves, but usually only when there were special guests. There might have been a specially sustaining drink, usually made with a honey and whisky base, one of which is known as 'auld man's milk', made with eggs and milk beaten together in the delft bowl, sweet-ened with honey and zested with whisky, brandy or rum, or they might have made the more substantial whisky, oatmeal and honey mix which has become known as 'Atholl brose'.

Though whisky was distilled from native barley, Highlanders were also familiar with other spirits, such as brandy and rum which were bartered from foreign luggers sailing into remote Highland sea lochs and exchanged, tax free, for salt herring and local cheese. The MacDougall larder was also augmented, in a similar way, with tea and coffee, oriental spices, dried figs, raisins, liquorice and sweet candies.

Like the Lowland cook at Ravelston, the Highland cook was dependent on her cauldron-broth for feeding the large – and often fluctuating – number of eaters who assembled daily in the great hall. It was an ideal food resource in the circumstances and became the most common day-to-day item in the Scottish diet, varying according to the location and wealth of the family. At Dunollie, the summer broth simmering over the slow-burning peat fire was rich with herbs, garlic, sorrel and watercress which were all growing wild for the picking. There were also tender young shoots of seaweed which could be gathered when the tide ebbed. The seeds which were sent from Glasgow in March had grown in the enclosed castle garden into cabbages, carrots, parsnips, turnips, beetroot, parsley and radishes. There was no shortage of meat, or well-hung game in the cellar, as well as salted, smoked and dried meat and fish hanging from rafters.

The scrag ends, bones and skinned head from a deer carcass were put into the pot and left to simmer for several hours. Then the rich liquid was strained off into one of the large 'potts'. Some

Eighteenth-century horn spoons, the common eating utensil of the time.

barley was added for thickening. Thin collops (slices) of venison from the haunch were fried in butter in the copper skillet until well browned before being tipped into the thickened broth. Just before it was served, some chopped sorrel and syboes (spring onions) were added to the broth; the sharpness of the sorrel balancing the richness of the dark brown gamy soup-stew. The meat from the cheeks – a great delicacy – was picked from the cooked head and put into the large pot, then served up in the centre of the table as the focal point of the meal.

Beside it, were the cold remains of a boiled salmon, some soft barley bannocks cooked on the girdle, butter, sheep's milk cheese, a large bowl of fresh cream to mix with newly-picked wild berries. Depending on the success of the hunters, there might have been a partridge, grouse, hare, mallard, woodcock or snipe turning and roasting on the spit.

While this kind of plentiful food supply and satisfying eating tradition existed until the eighteenth century, the clan system of provisioning was coming to an end. Even the clan chiefs were not wealthy in money terms. The total value of the house contents when Iain Ciar died was only £50, while the laird of Ravelston could afford to buy a single item of furniture costing £200.

There were no financial resources to support the Jacobite MacDougalls, whose castle and lands were confiscated when Iain Ciar was exiled for thirteen years in France and finally imprisoned. When he returned to the ownership of Dunollie Castle, his lands were still confiscated and for the last ten years of his life, until he died in 1737, he lived with his wife and children at the castle, dependent on their own, rather than the extended clan's efforts, to survive.

While the plenty of the past had been created by a system which made use of all the natural assets of land and sea by a judicious pooling of manpower and resources, future developments

Fish hanging to dry in a cottage kitchen in Foula, Shetland, 1902 - a centuries-old Highland and Island tradition. SEA

not only destroyed this system, but also created a new one which greatly affected the diet of the people. Heavy investment, such as was common in nineteenth-century Lowland agriculture, was pointless in the poorer environment of the non-arable Highlands. Instead, much of the land was used for rearing sheep or later bought as sporting estates, and the potential for continuing to grow native crops, rear hardy cattle and develop the traditional dairy industry was not realized.

Oatmeal retained its importance in the Highland diet. As part of the general system of mixing meal in a bowl to make a brose, the Highlanders' habit was to experiment with local ingredients. While day-to-day brose mixes relied mainly on meal and water the legendary 'Atholl brose' mix made with whisky, honey and oatmeal developed as a result, so the story goes, of a fifteenth-century Lord of the Isles who was causing trouble for the Scottish king.

Virtual monarchs in their island domain, with a strong fleet of galleys and a parliament in Islay, the Lord of the Isles was a continual menace to the authority of Scotland's kings. Around 1475 a rebellion broke out against King James III headed by the then Lord of the Isles, Iain Macdonald. The earls of Ross, Crawford and Atholl were sent to suppress the rebels. While Crawford commanded the sea forces, Atholl was sent to guard the land.

It was Atholl who finally captured the troublemaker on Skye. His spies noted a drinking well in a rock which he and his soldiers used every day. Many quarts of whisky were mixed into oatmeal and sweetened with heather honey and one night the water was removed from the well and replaced with 'Atholl' brose. The scheme worked, the rebels were captured, and Atholl was paid with the land and forests of Clunie, in a Charter (dated 1480) for his 'singular service and expenses in suppressing Iain, Lord of the Isles'.

Legend can obscure fact, and though the Atholl family have given their name to the brose it is unlikely that they actually invented the brose concoction. Their recipe was obviously a winning mix, and their use highly original, but a mealy brose, which was daily fare for the people, mixed with the national drink of the country, and flavoured with a naturally available sweetener is likely to have been a popular mix without the Atholl family's exploits.

Other parts of the country made other mixtures based on the three flavours, but combined in different ways. Sometimes cream was added. Coming in frozen from the hill, Gaelic-speaking Highlanders may mix themselves something which they call a *cromack*, sometimes pronounced *gromack*. A *cromag's-fu* being the quantity of oatmeal which can be lifted when the fingers and thumb are brought together. The meal is put into a mug or bowl and whisky, honey and cream added according to needs and taste.

Atholl brose

Recipe, published by the Atholl family and drunk by Queen Victoria when she visited Blair Atholl in 1844

To make a quart, take four dessert-spoonfuls of run honey and four sherry glassfuls of prepared oatmeal; stir these well together and put in a quart bottle; fill up with whisky; shake well before serving. To prepare the oatmeal, put it into a basin and mix with cold water to the consistency of thick paste. Leave for about half an hour, pass through a fine strainer, pressing with the back of a wooden spoon so as to leave the oatmeal as dry as possible. Discard the meal and use the creamy liquor for the brose.

There is also *stapag*, which can take many forms, but is sometimes made of cream, oatmeal, whisky and wild honey.

3 Old Edinburgh taverns

While Edinburgh's social life in its old medieval walled town continued to revolve around the communal tavern, there were also new developments in the social structure of the city. Burns was in his twenties and the future novelist Scott still a child when the New Town was being built across the North Bridge in the 1770s. Meanwhile the cramped and disorderly overhanging tenement lands of the High Street and Canongate continued to house every social class, who passed one another on the common stair. The old taverns provided a communal eating and drinking venue

A pewter 'tappit hen' and a smaller 'mutchkin', of the kind commonly used in taverns in the eighteenth century.

where the population could escape from their restricted living quarters.

It was common for all members of a family to frequent them at some point during the day or night and many ate tavern suppers every night of the week. They were the essence of simple hospitality: chairs and tables arranged in a plain room with an open coal fire for heat in an iron grate. A kettle of hot water swung from an iron chain over the fire, a cluster of tallow candles in a wooden chandelier hung from the ceiling. Shelves on the walls were for spent bottles. Hooks were for various jugs and drinking vessels such as tappit hens, chopins and mutchkins. There was no idle ornament or decoration. Every tavern had a number of similar rooms, some windowless, some partitioned with screens of thick brown paper to give visual privacy at least.

In one of the dining rooms there would be cheap tripe suppers, while in another boiling hot pennyworths of black and white puddings along with hot pies and kail (broth) suppers. In the most expensive dining room a roast turned on the spit, carved to order. A young boy would turn up for hot water to mix a bowl of brose. There might have been an old beggar at the doorway chewing on a hard, dried and salted spelding (haddock). Most of the two thousand odd hospitality houses were not only sources of refreshment, but also hummed during the day and night with the city's business affairs as merchants traded, patients consulted doctors, and men of the law argued their cases. They were mostly run by cheery landladies known as 'luckies'.

Though oysters were a cheap food sold in the streets by fishwives, they were also an important part of tavern eating. Down

Fish Market Close a number of taverns sold mainly oysters. This relatively new development had caught the mood of the town, allowing parties of well-bred women to join in the night's entertainment of singing and dancing, gambling and drinking, while consuming live oysters. Fresh from Newhaven, the large opened 'natives' were piled on a round wooden board in the centre of the table, with vinegar and pepper in cruets and plates of buttered bread. Drams of gin (whisky was still a Highlander's drink) and pots of porter were drunk throughout the night until the final warming draught of hot punch was served up before the party disbanded for the night.

The poet Robert Fergusson (1750-74) immortalized the taverns in his poem 'Caller Oysters', which captured the spirit of the town and its tavern culture:

> Auld Reikie's sons blyth faces wear;
> September's merry month is near,
> That brings in Neptune's caller cheer,
> New oysters fresh;
> The halesomest and nicest gear
> O'fish or flesh...
>
> Whan big as burns the gutters rin,
> Gin ye hae catcht a droukit skin,
> To luckie Middlemist's loup in,
> And sit fu' snug
> Owre oysters and a dram o' gin
> Or haddock lug.

Other tavern specialities could be found down Flesh Market Close, where sparerib steaks were cooked by the luckies whose husbands traded as butchers in the market. In the noisy tavern their fires glowed from morning to night. Gridirons clattered, beef steaks sizzled and customers waited in anticipation as wooden trenchers were rushed through steaming with crisp browned and juicy meat.

21

Walter Geikie's 'a merry meeting' captures the atmosphere of tavern conviviality.

It was a tavern-eating scene which caught the poetic imagination of Robert Burns when he arrived on his first visit to the Auld Toun in 1786 to work on the second edition of his poems with his publisher. The literati were keen to have his company at their elegant dinners, but Burns preferred the social mix of the tavern where the Lord Provost could be found sitting next to the humble caddie (porter). And it was in the taverns that he found inspiration for the bawdy lyrics, unfit for publication, which captured the riotous spirit of the age. The tavern fare was more to his taste too. Particularly at Dowie's (his favourite), where the food was noted for its fine quality. Along with some excellent Edinburgh ale, there was a gamey dish of jugged hare and rich apple pie, flavoured with lemon and cinnamon, raisins, almonds and some finely chopped lemon and orange peel. And later in the evening there would be plates of toast and cheese, known as a 'rarebit', the tangy cheese mix made by melting some ripe hard cheese on a plate in the hot hearth and mixing it with ale and a secret spicing while the bread was toasted in front of glowing coals.

It was not the kind of *hamely* fare which Burns was accustomed to. Broth, porridge and brose, hard oatcakes and ripe cheeses were more familiar daily food. Yet the tavern fare was not pretentious. Presentation was not considered important, it was the taste which mattered. Good-tasting food, which came from pots, or was roasted on spits, or grilled over hot coals, was served up – by twentieth century standards – in a rough-and-ready way. Long-boned chops of mutton were grasped from the broth pot and chewed unceremoniously. Slices of meat were carved off spit-roasts and eaten with fingers, potatoes were also hand-held. Communal eating from the pot continued, two eaters might sup from the same bowl of broth.

Shortly after Burns arrived in Edinburgh, an Ayrshire friend, Andrew Bruce, invited him to a family supper. Bruce's wife had made some haggis puddings for the supper using the pluck (innards) of the sheep, which she had bought from the Flesh Market. She had boiled, chopped and stuffed the sheeps' stomach bags full of the meat, oatmeal, onions and flavourings and they ate them that night, not with tatties (potatoes) and neeps (turnips) which were a meal in themselves, but by delving into the aromatic mix with a horn spoon while washing it down with some Edinburgh ale.

It is possible that this occasion may have been the inspiration for 'The Address to the Haggis', one of the few poems which Burns wrote during this first visit to Edinburgh. It appeared in the 1786 December issue of the *Caledonian Mercury* and in the January issue of the *Scots Magazine*. Choosing to celebrate a stuffed sheep's pudding, symbol of peasant thrift and ingenuity, Burns created a national eating institution, synonymous with values of sense and worth which he considered important in the Scots character.

Before he captured it for the Scots, haggis had been a common dish in England as well as in other continental countries. It appears originally in ancient Greece, the entrails of a sheep stuffed into the stomach bag. Yet from now on it was to became distinc-

A Good Scotch Haggis

Make the haggies-bag perfectly clean; parboil the draught; boil the liver very well, so as it will grate; dry the meal before the fire; mince the draught and a pretty large piece of beef very small; grate about half of the liver; mince plenty of suet, and some onions small; mix all these materials very well together, with a handful or two of the dried meal; spread them on the table, and season them properly with salt and mixed spices; take any of the scraps of beef that is left from mincing, and some of the water that boiled the draught, and make about a choppin of good stock of it; then put all the haggies-meat into the bag, and that broath in it; then sew up the bag; but be sure to put out all the wind before you sew it quite close. If you think the bag is thin, you may put it in a cloth. If it is large haggies, it will take at least two hours boiling.

tively Scottish, inextricably linked with the celebration of Burns's birthday. The first Burns Suppers took place in the early nineteenth century and have continued, not only in Scotland, but around the world in immortal memory of the universal poet.

An early recipe for haggis comes from Susanna MacIver's *Cookery and Pastry. As taught and practised by Mrs MacIver, teacher of those arts in Edinburgh.* First published in 1773 and printed in Edinburgh, it was written at her pupils' request and was part of a general development in printed cookery books around this time. Susanna MacIver had begun her professional cooking by making and selling jams, chutneys, pickles and cakes and later she ran a cookery school for the well-to-do. She sold her cookery book privately from her house in Stephens Law's Close.

4 New cosmopolitan elegance

The conflict between Old and New Edinburgh was not just in habits, manners and speech, but also in eating traditions as the population began to shift out of the Old Town. The old camaraderie of the tenement houses, howffs and taverns of the original medieval centre was in total contrast to the New Town of spacious classical houses and symmetrical squares and circuses. The

Quantities of food of all kinds were commonly sold in the street in the eighteenth and nineteenth centuries. Behind the apple barrow is a fishwife with her creel of fish. Walter Geikie

traditions of old cooking pots hanging over open fires, the oyster parties and tavern suppers, were threatened by the New Town's cosmopolitan elegance, though some believed that the old ways were worth preserving.

Burns had died in 1796 and Scott had taken up the Scottish cause. He worried that there should be a merging of Scotland with England; an un-Scotching, a loss of distinctive character, a failure to continue using the Scots language, all of which, he judged, would make the country boring and dull. Around him in Edinburgh he saw a city dividing into Old and New. Rich classes were moving out of the crowded tenement lands and into elegant new houses. A large part of the old was devastated by a fire in Parliament Square in 1824 and the modernists thought it no bad thing that social life should move out of the cramped tavern and into a more comfortable hotel in the New Town. They opposed Scott's nationalist zeal and his passion for the feudalistic romance of times long gone.

Scott, however, had the storyteller's skill and had caught the public imagination. He had also judged, rightly, that when a country's nationhood is at stake, the need to establish the traditions of the country become even stronger. As he gathered around him a set of lively spirits to celebrate Scottish history and traditions, their choice of eating illustrates a strong attachment to the old cauldron broths, the meats roast and boiled, the oysters, the beefsteaks, the tripe suppers and the haggis.

Scott still followed the old pattern of eating. Up early before six, he wrote or spent some time with the men discussing estate business before returning between eight and nine for the large breakfast which Lockhart describes in his biography:

> His table was always provided, in addition to the usual plentiful articles of a Scottish breakfast with some solid article, on which he did most lusty execution – a round of beef – a pastry – or, most welcome of all, a cold sheep's head, the charms of which primitive dainty he has so gallantly defended against the disparaging sneers of Dr Johnson. A huge brown loaf flanked his elbow, and it was placed upon a broad wooden trencher, that he might cut and come again with the bolder knife... He never tasted anything more before dinner, and dinner he ate sparingly.

Like most men he left luncheon to the fashionable ladies of the day who thought it an attractive diversion. It allowed them to push the dinner hour later into the evening but the men stayed loyal to the old ways. Every day about noon they would make their way through the narrow wynds of the old town, which continued to be the workplace of lawyers and businessmen around the law courts and Parliament buildings of the High Street, towards Lucky Fykie's in the Potterrow.

'Hoo d'ye do, mem?' the elderly and distinguished lawyers and bankers would say, as they entered the spick-and-span shop-cum-tavern run by Mrs Flockhart, the lucky who had made something of a name for her fykie (neat and clean) habits. In a small room to the front she had laid out on a bunker seat in the window a bottle of whisky and one of both rum and brandy, flanked by a number of glasses. The only eating during this midday break were the ginger biscuits, known as Parliament cakes (parlies) which she served on a salver.

No money changed hands but every month or so they would 'settle up', paying for what they had eaten and drunk. The elderly men enjoyed their own version of the mid-day snack, whilst believing, like Scott, that lunch was a frivolity which had nothing to do with them.

Ginger parlies, which were as popular then as shortbread is today, were a kind of ginger 'bread', originally made with breadcrumbs, mixed with honey and ginger, rolled into a flat square shape, often with whole cloves stuck on top, and baked till very hard. Though the eleventh-century Crusaders introduced most other spices to Britain, it was the Romans who had originally brought ginger. Grown in their African colonies, they used it in massive quantities and by the fifteenth century both Scotland and England were addicted to the spice.

No annual fair was complete without its gingerbread booth. The hard, biscuit-gingerbread appearing in many novel shapes; king's and queen's crowns were covered in gold leaf, colourful ribbons, bows and streamers were used to attract the people who came to buy the fancy gingerbread shapes. Gingerbread was also sold in the streets by itinerant sellers. One, Robbie Salmond, an eccentric character who walked the streets of the Old Town around Mrs Flockhart's time, had his bizarre selling techniques recorded in an account of the street cries of Edinburgh. Gathering a crowd around him, they waited in anticipation for the moment they liked best when he tossed out samples of gingerbread with the shout 'Bullock's blood and sawdust! Feed the ravens! Feed the ravens!'

Among the 'Scott set' were a number of men who took the celebration of national eating traditions a step further. William Blackwood was a shrewd and intelligent man of middle age when he first published Blackwood's *Edinburgh Magazine* in 1817. It was a huge success, causing a stir and excitement in Edinburgh exceeding Blackwood's wildest dreams. One of the most popular columns, however, was the vivid, racy, imaginative talk, with much reference to the food, which took place between three half-fictitious characters who met of an evening in Ambrose's Tavern in Gabriel's Road in the New Town.   It had started one night, after a particularly amusing evening in the company of Blackwood and two young barristers, John Wilson and John Gibson Lockhart (Scott's son-in-law and later his biographer) when Lockhart declared that it was a pity that a shorthand writer had not been there to take down their conversation. Blackwood challenged him to write it up for the magazine and the first *Noctes Ambrosianae* column appeared in March 1822.

Later taken over completely by Wilson, who found it the perfect medium for his humorous, satirical style, he introduced the characters of the Ettrick Shepherd (based on Scott's friend, the poet and novelist James Hogg) and Timothy Tickler (based on his uncle, Robert Sym) plus himself with the pseudonym Christopher North. The rollicking manner of North, contrasted against the rural freshness of the Ettrick Shepherd's vernacular Scots dialogue, provided the leaven, while Tickler's conservative line prevented the two young bloods from becoming totally outrageous. The leading High Court judge of the day, Lord Cockburn, described North's dialogues as 'bright with genius', his interpretation of Hogg's Scots language as the 'best Scotch written in modern times'.

The preference of the *Noctes* epicures was not the new formal dinners with their 'corner' dishes of ragouts and fricassées etc. 'I like,' said the Shepherd, 'to bring the haill power o' my stamach to bear on vittles that's worthy o't, and no fritter't awa on side dishes, sic as pâtés and trash o' that sort.'

The well-filled ashets of 'roast and boiled' were enough of an attraction in themselves, they thought. Placed, all at once on the table, to avoid the interruption of 'instalments', they enjoyed a wide repertoire of dishes cooked by 'douce, civil, judicious' Ambrose, the cook. They liked mustard with their steaks, apple sauce and mashed potatoes with their roast goose; their turkey devilled, their potatoes mealy, their cheese well-ripened and toasted, their mince pies soaked with brandy and set alight, their oysters by the hundred.

The Shepherd describes the national broths:

That's hotch-potch – and that's cocky-leeky – the twa best soups in natur. Broon soup's moss-water – and white soup's like scaudded

Late eighteenth- and nineteenth-century table ware. On the right are examples of the popular Wemyss ware, made in Kirkcaldy.

milk wi' worms in't. But see, sirs, hoo the ladle stauns o' itsel in the potch – and I wish Mr Tickler could see himsel the noo in a glass, curlin up his nose, wi' his een glistenin, and his mouth watering, at the sight and smell o' the leeky.

While Scott and the *Noctes* set enthused over old traditions, a minor novelist and editor, Christian Isobel Johnstone, chose to write (anonymously) about Scottish food in the most successful cookery book of the century. In *The Cook and Housewife's Manual* by Margaret (Meg) Dods, she uses the fictitious Meg Dods, a character in Scott's novel *St Ronan's Well*, as the author, describing her style of cooking and the inauguration of the gastronomic Cleikum Club, in a lively introduction in the style of Scott's historical fiction, which some have argued may have been written by him. There is, however, no evidence for this, but her lively style extends into the recipes .

To Serve Oysters in the Shell

Let the opener stand behind the eater's chair, who should make a quick and clean conveyance. So placed, wash, brush and open and beard the oysters, and arrange them on rows on a tray; or if pinched for room, heap the shells in piles; the fresher from the sea, and the more recently opened the better. The French serve lemon-juice with raw oysters; we serve this or vinegar, pepper and toasted crusts.

Ginger Parlies

With two pounds of the best flour dried, mix thoroughly one pound of good brown sugar and a quarter-pound of ground ginger. Melt a pound of fresh butter, add to it one of treacle, boil this, and pour it on the flour; work up the paste as hot as your hands will bear it, and roll it out in very large cakes, the sixth of an inch thick or less; mark it in squares with a knife or paper-cutter, and fire in a slow oven. Separate the squares while soft, and they will soon get crisp.

Meg Dods
The Cook and Housewife's Manual 1826

5 The fishing tradition

While the novels of Lowlander Scott were responsible for popularizing the historical romance of be-tartaned Highlanders, the Gaelic-speakers of the North had moved on from previous Jacobite aspirations. In many areas bankrupt clan chieftains had sold their lands. In others, they had turned to sheep-rearing. The resulting Clearances in the nineteenth century marked the end of the communal clan system where the produce of land and sea had been a common asset. The system of grazing domestic animals on the hills during the summer became less and less practical, and salmon, deer and grouse became sport for the new landowners.

While in the remoter areas of the Highlands and Islands sea fishing continued to be an important part of the peasant-crofters economy, from the 1840s to the 1880s the fishing industry on the East Coast was particularly prosperous. Three men would work in one yawl. Sailing to the fishing grounds, they took with them a keg of water and enough oatcakes and cheese in their *pocken mor* (canvas bag with a drawstring) to keep them going for twenty-four hours. The baited line was cast and left for half an hour before being pulled in, hopefully full of cod, haddock, mackerel, whiting, cuddies (young coalfish), soles, flounders, skate and dogfish. As one man rowed another pulled in the line while a third removed the fish as they came into the boat.

Boy with a dish of stuffed fish-heads, Lewis, 1950s.

Back on the shore, the catch was laid out on the beach and the three men distributed piles of fish evenly between them. Their wives took on the job of packing the fish into creels which they then put onto their backs to go off selling around the country.

A fishwife selling to a customer in Corstorphine, outside Edinburgh, early 1900s. She would have brought her fish by tram from Newhaven or Musselburgh. SEA

Not all the fish, however, was sold fresh. Each fishwife was also an expert smoker, owning a wooden smoking shed with an earthen floor and a hollow centre where the fire was laid. There was no chimney, so as the fire burned, the shed filled with smoke. Along with her collection of hard woods, she used fir cones to make the cool smoke which preserved the fish. Firstly, however, the fish had to be gutted, split and their heads removed. Haddock was most commonly smoked by this method. Then they had to be scrubbed clean of blood and put into a tub with salt to preserve them. Finally they were hung up on spits and put into the smoking shed. The process took the best part of the day. The fishwife smoked for two days of the week and for the other four, went to the country selling fish. On Sunday she went to church.

This method of smoking fish by splitting open was common practice in most East Coast fishing communities, eventually taking its name Finnan (haddie) from the Aberdeenshire fishing village of Findon, colloquially known as Finnan. Further south, a 'closed' unsplit cure also developed at Auchmithie, a small fishing village just north of Arbroath. Here, the fish became known as a Smokie, not smoked in a tall shed with cool smoke but over a hotter fire in a half whisky barrel covered with layers of hessian sacking.

Gutted and salted, a pair of fish, their tails tied together, were hung over wooden rods. Layers of sacking were laid on top. The smoking process took about forty minutes, which cooked the fish to a coppery brown on the outside, flavouring the flesh with a mild smokiness. Both finnans and smokies (which were later smoked also in Arbroath and became known as Arbroath smokies) joined the collection of wet fish in the fishwife's creel.

A Caithness kippering house, around 1900. SEA

The day was not ended for this intrepid fishwife when she returned to her family at night after her day's work. While the best of the catch had been sold, there were always enough small flounders, whitings and a few wings of skate to make a 'fry'. Not fried in a pan, but grilled on a brander on a good 'red' fire, they were eaten with butter (exchanged for fish at the farm) and floury boiled potatoes.

There were also other foods which came from the country to supplement the fisher-families' feeding: cheese, meal, fruits and vegetables in season, eggs and occasionally a piece of venison. The creel filled up with food supplies for her family in an economic system which depended little on monetary wealth. Butchermeat was not as plentiful as fish, but trap-caught rabbits, poached fish and game as well as the odd wild cormorant, tasting of wild duck, were often found in the broth pot.

But undoubtably the most common item was her own smoked haddock. Put into the large black pot along with some onions, she covered everything with water and left it to simmer until the fish was cooked. Before she left for the day's toil she removed the pot from the fire and boiled up some potatoes. By the time she had returned at night someone in the family would have removed the fish bones and skin and peeled the potatoes. Then the potatoes were mashed and mixed into the flaked fish and its stock, with some milk added to make it into a not-too-thick and not-too-runny mixture. The fishwives soup/stew, known by the Scots word 'skink', became identified with the town of Cullen when the food historian, F M McNeill, included the recipe in her collection of folk recipes *The Scots Kitchen* (1929).

Because line-caught fish was so plentiful, there was not much need for foraging on the shore for shellfish though cockles and whelks were eaten and cuvie (a rope-like tangle) was peeled and eaten raw. They also gathered dulse which was dry-roasted on the brander until crisp, or put into a broth for flavour. Caragean was dried and used to thicken milk, making a solid jelly which was eaten with thick cream.

The only method of baking was on the girdle, where soft barley bannocks were made, large, round and thick. Hard oatcakes, triangular and thinner, were a staple sustenance, eaten with slices of butter or cheese; some children ate them with a slice of boiled turnip (swede) from the broth pot.

For festivities there was clootie dumpling, a festive dish common throughout the rest of the country. A pudding boiled in a cloth (clootie), the dumpling's contents depended on the fortunes of the family; if times were hard it would contain only flour, suet and some spice and soda, while in times of plenty it was a richer affair made with sugar, syrup, black treacle, dried fruit and spices.

To make the dumpling, the mixture was put into a large square piece of

A herring gutter at Nairn in the 1920s. The gutters worked at enormous speed, packing three barrels with gutted and salted herring in an hour. SEA

cloth which had been boiled, then dusted with a thin coating of flour. It was tied up loosely to allow it to expand and put into a pot of boiling water where it was cooked gently for about four hours. When it was ready to be turned out, it was dipped in cold water for a minute to loosen the skin, before the cloth was removed and the turned-out dumpling put in front of the fire to 'dry off' and develop its characteristic skin. Cut in slices and eaten hot, it was usually sprinkled with sugar or later eaten cold. The next day it might be fried with bacon and egg for breakfast.

In summer there was herring. The men, who went to sea with nets, were followed around the country by the women-gutters as the herring shoals moved throughout the season. Women gutted, packed and salted millions of fish a year into barrels which were largely exported to Russia and Scandinavia. But all coastal-living crofter-fishermen throughout the Highlands and Islands also salted their own herring for winter use.

On the West Coast, where much of the grazing lands had been lost, the fisher-crofter people also relied heavily for their feeding on the patch of potatoes which they grew on their small strips of cultivated land. In a similar way to the Irish, the people came to depend on potatoes as the staple carbohydrate in their diet, its main agricultural advantage being that it grew underground where it could not be damaged by wind and rain.

If they caught a netful of herring in the summer, when the loch filled with shoals of the fish, they would make their own salt her-rring, traditionally eaten with potatoes, and forming the basis of a staple meal which Alexander Stewart describes as a typical but-and-ben dish in *Nether Lochaber* (1883).

The other day, landing from our boat, we went into a cottar's house just as the gudewife was preparing the family dinner. A pot of new potatoes was boiling on the fire. Looking now and again into the pot, and listening with inclined ear to the sound, actually musical in such a case, of its boiling and bubbling, she was ready at the proper instant to snatch it off the fire, and carrying it to the corner of the kitchen she poured off the water and immediately re-hung it over the fire, shortening the chain by which it was suspended by a link or two, that the fire might not, now that it was waterless, have too much effect upon it. She then got some half-dozen fresh herrings, caught early that morning – herrings large, beautiful and as silvery-scaled as a salmon – and drying them nicely with a cloth, she placed them flatwise, side by side, on the top of the potatoes in the pot, the lid of which she was careful to fit tightly by means of a coarse kitchen towel, which served at once to cover the contents and to cause the lid to fit so tightly steam was effectually retained.

During a quarter of an hour, perhaps, the wife kept an attentive eye on the pot, never once lifting the lid, however, but from time to time raising or lowering a link in the chain as in her judgment was necessary. All being ready at last, she took the pot off the fire and set it on a low stool in the middle of the floor. She then lifted the lid and the cloth, and the room was instantly filled with a savoury steam that made one's mouth water merely to inhale it.

Occupying each a low chair, we were invited to fall to, to eat without knife or fork, or trencher, just with our fingers out of the pot as it stood. It was a little startling, but only for a moment. After a word of grace we dipped our hand into the pot and took out a potato, hot and mealy, and with another we took a nip out of the silvery flank of the herring nearest us. It was a mouthful for a king, sir!

6 Urban plenty and want

With the growth of industrialization, and the movement of people from the country into towns, the feeding habits of all classes of the population changed in quite dramatic ways. For the urban middle classes, as the opulent era of the Victorian Empire drew to a close, a lifestyle which had depended on cheap domestic labour began to change. When they were no longer able to employ a cook in the kitchen, there was no longer so much time and effort spent on cooking. Elaborate presentations of food and time-consuming procedures declined. Victorian showiness and affluent eating became not only unpractical but also unfashionable.

A highly-decorated Scottish-made 'saut bucket' dated 1854.

Feeding in rich houses, however, suffered no lack of resources and affluent eating continued in much the same manner as it had in the past. Eating might begin with a large breakfast, laid out on a long mahogany sideboard, of perhaps five courses plus tea, toast and preserves. There would be a first course of eggs followed by bacon and then a fish course, a roast platter consisting of chops, steaks or sausages, with the

POTAGES

POTAGES
De faisan aux quenelles
Purée de choux-fleurs

POISSONS
Cabillaud aux oeufs
Merlans frits

ENTREES
Mousse de jambon aux concom-bres
Pojarky de volaille

RELEVES
Boeuf rôti
Choux braisés
Kallre Nuszmet Ralm

ROTI
Dinde farcie

ENTREMETS
Les haricots verts sautés
Les choux de Bruxelles au beurre
Spurutx Gebacknes

LE DESSERT

SIDEBOARD
Hot and cold chicken
Boiled Tongue
Cold roast beef
Salad

final choice from the game course. Lunch was a lighter affair, but a dinner of any pretensions would have required at least eight courses.

In the style of the day, it would have followed the French pattern. Ideally, a French chef would be in the kitchen. On her last visit to Balmoral before she died, Queen Victoria's dinner on Tuesday 9 October 1900, cooked by her French chefs, is shown on the left. This was modest by Buckingham Palace standards, where dinner usually started with four soups, four fish dishes, four removes and eight entrées. After a break for some water ice to rest the stomach came a choice of three roasts, six removes and fifteen desserts. It was a style of eating which set the fashion for French food among the upper classes, with its most popular expression in the grand hotels of the Edwardian era where French food cooked by a French chef was *de rigueur*.

In influential kitchens throughout the UK, classical French dishes replaced national traditions as menus were written in French, and aspiring young cooks learned to make elaborate mousses, soufflés and rich creamy sauces. It was a style which was to last through two world wars and into the 1980s before a more sensible approach prevailed and the rich *cuisine classique* was ousted by the more moderate *nouvelle cuisine* as leading chefs took on the business of simplifying their style by using less cream and butter, and concentrated more on the natural flavours of quality ingredients, perfectly cooked (see chapter 9).

But for the urban deprived, the early twentieth century was a difficult time for food. Not only were the effects of deprivation starting to be noticed in everyday food, but also the food-manufacturing industry was beginning to influence the way people ate to a much larger extent. Standardization throughout the country, as a result of modern food-processing techniques, was threatening many of the distinctive local and national food traditions. The contrast was made by the distinguished dietician Lord Boyd Orr when he pointed out that with the introduction of machinery '...natural foodstuffs have been changed into artificial foodstuffs, with the very substances purified away that the Almighty put there to keep us in perfect health.' Joining him in the fight to preserve the quality of national food traditions and regional foods, which were clearly in danger of falling into oblivion, the folklorist and historian, F M McNeill, set about researching traditional and local dishes from Shetland to the Borders and the collection was published in 1929 as *The Scots Kitchen*.

The urban poor's feeding moved from a healthy rural diet, based on oatmeal and milk, to what is now known as a nutritionally deprived diet based on tea, white bread and processed food. Just before McNeill's book was published, there had been a series of Hunger Marches, after the General Strike of 1926, which illustrated most vividly the plight of those at the bottom of the heap. For them, the kettle of boiling water had replaced the cooking-pot broths. Pots of tea, infusing on black iron hobs, where once fragrant brews had simmered and stewed, were the norm. In Dundee, for instance, where the jute industry employed cheap female labour, unemployed men who did all the domestic work became known as 'kettle bilers'.

In their cramped tenements, one room might be the bedroom, parlour, kitchen and scullery. In the worst living conditions, an upturned tea chest might be their table, some empty tin cans their only drinking vessels. A 'Poor Relief' handout was two pounds of jam and a loaf of bread. Their traditional oatmeal was more expensive than a loaf of bread, which required no cooking. Tea

Mallaig harbour on a Saturday morning in the mid-1930s.
The fishermen are buying ice cream sliders from a barrow. SEA

and sugar for a warming cup of tea had become a cheap form of available sustenance. The lack of cooking at home, however, was compensated to some extent by the food which they bought in the streets, ready-cooked.

The street kerb was their club. Most of the street food at this time came from barrow-pushing Italian immigrants who made delicious ice cream in summer and warming fried chips and roasted chestnuts in winter. At the Greenmarket in Dundee, the chip stall was a covered tent owned by a Belgian, Eduard de Gernier, who sold a poke of salt-and-vinegared chips for a penny. There was also the 'buster' stall where they sold saucers of hot peas and vinegar at a sit-down bench and table. The barrow-pushing

The kitchens at Stirling Castle have been set up to replicate an early sixteenth-century scene. Game, fish and a range of vegetables are among the ingredients.

Essential utensils of the traditional Scottish kitchen: the pot for making broth, the girdle for baking and the bannock spade for turning bannocks, the brander for grilling, and a wooden saut bucket which would be placed handily near the hearth. Broth or porridge was eaten out of a wooden bowl with a horn spoon.

Highland Cottage, Inverness-shire, 1847. K J Ellice

Breakfast at Glenquoich Lodge, Inverness-shire, 1847. K J Ellice

The kitchen at Castle Fraser. The iron pots were the main vessels for cooking until at least the eighteenth century, and later in remoter parts of Scotland.

A corner of the kitchen of a Glasgow tenement, a typical interior of between the wars. The National Trust for Scotland's Tenement House.

A late twentieth-century Halloween in the kitchen of the Shaw family, South Queensferry. A turnip lantern reminding us of the importance of neeps in the Scottish diet. John Shaw. SEA

A fishmonger's slab in Edinburgh. In the 1990s exotic species – tuna and parrot fish – mingle with the more traditional smoked and fresh haddock.

Traditional Scottish foods along with more recent manifestations of a Scottish identity in food and drink.

Late twentieth-century trends as significant in Scotland as elsewhere: the growing number of vegetarians and interest in health foods; and the availability of ready-cooked food a phone-call away.

ice cream makers sold their ice cream, firstly from penny-lick glasses, before cones and wafers became a more hygienic method, the ice cream usually coated in a red raspberry sauce known as 'Tally's blood'. Fourpenny-specials, sold in sit-down cafes in the Overgate, were concocted in large fluted sundae glasses, filled with layers of flavoured ices, preserved fruits and topped with fancy wafers. 'Het peys' (Scotch hot-pies) and 'bridies' (Forfar bridies, see page 72) came from Wallaces in the Vaults.

The Scotch pie was a development of the early raised pie, made with hot-water paste and 'raised' up the side of a mould, then left to set and harden before the filling was added. The Scotch pie is made in the same way, though as an individual-portion size pie. Made by local bakers, itinerant pie-men or -women, or by tavern cooks, the 'hot-pie' became a sustaining hand-held convenience food for working men, women and children. It was eaten hot, or reheated at home, and some bakers also provided a jug of hot gravy for pouring into the centre of the pie. Tinned beans and mashed potatoes became popular 'fillers' piled up in the space above the meat filling which was originally minced mutton.

The renowned pie-maker in Glasgow was known as 'Granny Black', whose tavern in the Candleriggs became Mecca for pie-lovers around the turn of the century. Though sold today from all bakeries on a daily basis, the 'hot-pie' trade moves into mass-production on Saturdays as they are delivered by the thousand to football grounds for eating at half-time, with a cup of hot bovril.

From the early chip stalls, there developed the Chip Shop or 'Chippie'. They were already well-established in London and the North of England and the Scots-Italians were largely responsible for the growth in Scotland of one of the mainstays of the urban diet throughout the rest of the twentieth century. In Scotland the favoured fried fish was haddock, as it remains today.

While the standard of living may have fluctuated according to the resources of the family, the dependence on ready-made foods and food retailers in an urban setting was now universal. The problems of feeding a growing urban population gave a new

Stone bottles and containers, including a ginger-beer bottle and a butter jar, nineteenth century.

impetus to the food industry, which from this period onwards grew in size and complexity.

Developments were aimed at new methods of preservation, since the holding and marketing of large quantities of highly perishable food was impractical. Initial attempts concentrated on the centuries-old method of drying and salting, but it was in the field of canning and refrigeration that new developments met with greatest success. It was a Scottish emigrant to Australia, James Harrison, who produced the first ice-making machine in 1850.

In addition to this completely new source of food supplies, the staples of bread, butter and milk were also developing new dimensions. The roller mill had been introduced about the middle of the nineteenth century and this, together with the use of silk gauze for sifting flour, led to a much finer flour from which the germ could be extracted. Semolina, custard powder and cornflour were the new by-products of this process, since the degree of crushing could be controlled and the coarser and finer particles separated more easily.

To overcome the problem of rancidity in butter, and also to help supply an increasing market, experimentation in France had led to the invention of 'butterine' or 'oleomargarine', later to become known as 'margarine'. Then there was the problem of supplying the urban population with highly perishable milk, which encouraged the commercial solutions of condensing, evaporating and drying, resulting in tins of condensed and evaporated milk and dried milk in powder form.

From now on, commercially prepared foods and cooked provisions from street vendors or cooked-food shops were essential to the mass of the population who could not feed themselves without this source of supply. Labouring children who left school at the statutory age of twelve, and whose mothers worked in a factory, would have depended to a large extent on cooked street food, bread and jam in the form of 'jellie pieces' along with hot sugary tea and a number of processed foods. Family-cooked meals at home would have depended largely on the state of the family finances, and on the availability of cooking facilities, as well as whether there was someone living at home with the time and effort to cook.

Scotland's tradition of sugar confectionery developed when shiploads of sugar from the West Indies sailed up the Clyde to be refined at Greenock, commonly known as Sugarapolis. Making a living from sweetie-boiling was a common occupation for itinerant people and small grocers in Scotland, and remnants of this tradition survive in native sweets such as tablet and toffee as well as a number of local sweeties.

In Kirriemuir Starry Rock survives in the back of a small sweetie shop in The Roods. A home-made buttery rock, made into small child's-hand-sized sticks, it is wrapped in wax paper in bundles of nine and made from a recipe handed down through many generations.

The dark brown peppermint boilings once known as Taffy Rock Bools, but now called Hawick Balls (the thing to suck at rugby matches in the Borders) were originally made and sold in Hawick by Jessie McVitie and Aggie Lamb in their shop in Drumlanrig Square around the 1850s. They also made Black Sticky Taffy with treacle and White Taffy with peppermint. The method was to hang the lump of hot boiled sugar on a nail on the wall beside the shop counter, watching out for it as it slowly stretched downwards towards the floor. Just as it was about to hit the ground it would be grabbed, twisted and hung over the nail again. This procedure was repeated several times until the sugar was properly 'pulled' and ready for chopping up into balls.

*A sweet stall at Leuchars air show in 1992 bears witness to
the survival of the Scottish 'sweet tooth'. Shaws have clearly
been in business for over a century.* Dorothy Kidd, SEA

As pleasurable sustenance, comfort, reward, enticement,
barter, as well as, of course, the language of love, sweeties are
consummate. Or, as Harry Lauder, once wrote to his favourite
sweetie maker about their Creamery Toffee: 'Your confection is
perfection.' This prompted the firm to make use of the accolade
from the great man on the lids of all their sweetie tins.

7 Native foods and culinary traditions

While in social conditions of extreme plenty, or extreme want,
native foods and culinary traditions had little chance of survival,
among the rural population they continued to thrive. Particularly
in the more remote areas of the country where the people were
less affected by the standardization of the food-processing industry and the power of a sophisticated food-retailing industry. In
rural lifestyles, girdle-baking and one-pot broths have continued

as an important part of the diet. The availablity of the raw materials, such as the native bere crop in Orkney, determined the survival of rural traditions linked to the land or sea. In Orkney beremeal continues to be made into bere bannocks by all the bakers.

This distinctive form of northern barley is known as 'bigg' or 'big' (*Hordeum vulgare*) which is called 'bere' (pronounced 'bare' in the far north). Despite the fact that today barley is mainly malted, and used for distilling whisky, this variety was the main cereal crop in Scotland for all purposes from neolithic times until the introduction of oats in the Roman period. From this time onwards, the oat crop developed but did not start to compete with barley until about the seventeenth century. By the eighteenth century, oatmeal had become the predominant food crop, and barley

The date is 1967, but bannocks are still being baked in the traditional way, on a girdle suspended over an open fire, in Turnabrain, Angus. The bannocks are turned with a bannock spade. SEA

was used mainly for distilling. In cooking, however, it retained its importance in barley broth and barley bannocks. In the Highlands and Islands and among the lower classes in the Lowlands, barley continued to be used for making bread, though this has largely died out.

It is not known where, or when, cultivated oats originated. The first evidence of the grain in Scotland is of carbonized grains, found at digs along the Forth and Clyde canal, dated a hundred or so years BC, but it is generally agreed that although oats thrive best in cool climates, they originally came from some warmer country in the East. In a cool climate, the growth is comparatively slow, which allows the kernels to fill out better and therefore have a better flavour (the reason Scottish-grown oatmeal is rated better than English). Oatmeal has the advantage over barley of being more versatile, with a greater range of 'cuts' (grades from coarse pinhead, the grain split in two, to fine flour) providing a variety of textures, made into staple items such as oatcakes, porridge, skirlie and brose.

By the end of the eighteenth century oatmeal had become firmly established as the peoples' grain: 'Oatmeal with milk, which they cook in different ways, is their constant food, three times a day, throughout the year, Sundays and holidays included,' says J Donaldson in *A General View of Agriculture of the Carse of Gowrie* (1794).

Eating porridge at Brownhill Farm, Auchterless, Aberdeenshire, 1959. Alexander Fenton, SEA

Throughout the nineteenth century its popularity increased. The figure of the penniless Scottish university scholar, surviving on his sack of oatmeal, is legendary. The mid-term holiday known as 'Meal Monday' was reputedly given to allow the student to return home to replenish his supply of oatmeal.

With the industrial revolution, and the rise of cheap white bread accompanied by tea, however, the old oatmeal traditions of porridge, brose and oatcakes were seriously under threat and in many cases tea and white bread became the staple diet to the detriment of the peoples' health (see Chapter 6). This was discovered most dramatically when Scottish men, undergoing medical examinations prior to signing up for service in World War I, were found to be undernourished and in such poor health that a high percentage were rejected as unfit for service. The fact that the oatmeal tradition has survived into the present century is largely due to a greater understanding of the value of oatmeal as a highly nutritious food and its role as a popular 'health' food of the latter part of the twentieth century.

Another old-established food which has had a considerable influence throughout the centuries on culinary traditions is the potato, widely used in traditional dishes such as broths, clapshot, rumbledethumps, stovies, potato scones and chappit tatties; also essential for eating with salt herring in traditional tatties and herring (see page 36).

There was a gradual acceptance of the potato in Scotland first as a garden crop, and later as a field crop, throughout the late eighteenth and early nineteenth century as a useful food supply, particularly in areas of impoverished peasantry and in some parts of the country it became as important as it was in Ireland. An account of the *Economic History of the Hebrides and Highlands* (1808) states that by about 1763, the people were subsisting on potatoes for nine months of the year. In Lowland areas, however, where the climate and soil was better, the diet was less dominated by potatoes. One estimate judged that they made up only about a third of the daily diet.

Being an underground crop, less susceptible to vagaries of climate, it had an advantage over grain crops, though there was still the risk of potato blight, a disease which caused the serious potato famine in Ireland and also a less devastating one in Scotland. Part of the potato's popularity was that it combined well with the northern Scot's staple diet of milk and fish. In a description of the diet in *Sketches and Tales of the Shetland Isles*, E Edmondston (1856) 'Fish with oat bread or potatoes, without any accompaniment at all, forms the three daily meals of the Shetland cottager.'

Traditionally, the Scots have always preferred a drier mealier potato with a stronger, more dominant flavour, specializing in varieties such as Golden Wonder and Kerr's Pinks, and those such as Duke of York and Champion which are no longer grown commercially. In the nineteenth century a common sight in city streets, were farm carts selling 'mealy tatties', which were simply dry floury potatoes boiled in salted water.

The Golden Wonder (1906) was raised by John Brown near Arbroath and it remains one of the varieties with the highest amount of dry matter. Kerr's Pink (1917) was raised by James Henry in 1907 and was known as Henry's Seedling until it won the Lord Derby Gold Medal at the Ormskirk Trials in 1916. Its merits were recognized by a seedsman (Mr Kerr) who bought the seed and renamed it Kerr's Pink in 1917. Though the amount grown of both varieties is not high, the demand remains and with the increased interest in potato varieties more attention has been paid to the qualities of such old traditional varieties.

Linking up with potatoes in native dishes, such as clapshot, is the neep (Swedish turnip, or swede, or rutabaga from the Swedish dialect name 'rotbagga'). Though the name 'turnip' is generally used in England for the white turnip (French *navet*) the Scots (and some Northern English) have adopted the word 'turnip' for their entirely different, but more commonly grown, swede.

While the Romans were responsible for introducing the English white turnip, *Brassica rapa,* the yellow turnip, *Brassica campestris* came to Scotland in the late eighteenth century. It was around this time that the pioneers of English agriculture were growing crops of turnips for feeding to cattle during the winter, thus enabling them to build up breeding herds when previously most of the animals had to be killed in the autumn. The Scots took to the yellow turnip as a vegetable for human consumption more enthusiastically than the English, who appear to have regarded it first and foremost as cattle-fodder. Only in some parts of Northern England and Scotland was it eaten with any enthusiasm. 'Our club [The Cleikum],' says Meg Dods (1826), 'put a little powdered gineger [sic] to their mashed turnips, which were studiously chosen of the yellow, sweet, juicy sort, for which Scotland is celebrated.'

Dressing potatoes at Davidson's Mains, near Edinburgh, 1912 or 1913. After riddling, to remove the very small potatos, the remainder were sorted and graded. SEA

In time, mashed turnips, or bashed neeps as they were known, became the traditional accompaniment to haggis at Burns Suppers (see page 24) along with mashed potatoes (chappit tatties). In the Islands and parts of the Highlands, where both potatoes and turnips were grown, they were often mixed together as the main course dish of the day in a peasant-style eating tradition which was largely devoid of meat. In Orkney the mixed potato and turnip dish became known as clapshot (origin unknown) now a common dish throughout the country, frequently eaten with haggis.

Originally a staple green winter vegetable, kail or kale survives well in the harsh Scottish winter since it has the rare quality in a vegetable of benefiting from periods of hard frost. It has no heart but grows on a long stem with curled, finely dented leaves, and its

Brian Wilson bringing home a bunch of kail, Fair Isle, Shetland, 1956. Alasdair Alpin MacGregor, SEA

flavour changes from mild to more intensely spicy after it has been frosted.

The kail-yard (kitchen garden) was to the Scots (particularly in the Lowlands, Highlanders used nettles as a green vegetable) what the potato-plot was to the Irish peasant. Kail became so inextricably linked with eating, that the midday meal became known as 'kail' and the bells of St Giles Cathedral in Edinburgh which chimed at dinner-time (in the eighteenth century at 2 o'clock) were known as the 'kail-bells'. Scotland is often referred to as the 'land o' kail' and 'kailyaird' has been applied to a school of nineteenth- and twentieth-century fiction, including J M Barrie and S R Crockett, which depicts Scottish village life.

While the Scots used the spelling kail, the Northern English called it 'cale'. Both names come from its generic name *borecole*, a brassica which was introduced by the Dutch, originally known as 'boerenkool'. Today, it is known in Scotland and the rest of the UK as either kail or kale and the Scots continue to use it in broths, or as a vegetable in its own right, while in England it has largely been used as winter feeding for cattle.

Leeks are the dominant vegetable in cock-a-leekie, a Lowland broth, originally made with mature cocks and leeks which has become a classic combination (see Chapter 4). Though leeks were grown in Scotland from the Middle Ages on, the first mention of cock-a-leekie is in the Ochtertyre House book (1737). Its success has depended to a large extent on the quality of leeks available and the dish is thought to have flourished, certainly in the eighteenth- and nineteenth-century Edinburgh taverns, as a direct result of the market-gardens which developed on the fertile soils along the Lothian coast, supplying the city with vegetables and fruits and becoming renowned for the fine quality of their leeks.

A variety of the common long winter leek, raised near Edinburgh and possessing a longer, thicker stem and broad leaves, is described as a '*poireau de Musselbourgh*' by William Robinson in *The Vegetable Garden* (1885) when he says that 'the fine qualities of this vegetable are much better known to the

Welsh, Scotch and French than to the English or Irish'. Scots leeks continue to be distinguished from other leeks, particularly by their long leaf (green flag) and short blanch (white). The large amount of green is necessary to give broths a good green colour. A traditional Scottish leek will have almost as much green as white, while 'long blanched' leeks with only a very short green flag are more typically English.

Because it is sweeter and more delicate than the onion, it is often described as the 'king of the soup onions'. Small to medium sized leeks have the sweetest flavour. The Musselburgh leek, a leek grown for winter hardiness, though no longer used commercially, continues to be grown by some amateur gardeners.

Stovies
A Cottage Recipe

Potatoes	salt and pepper
onions	dripping, water

The old-fashioned iron saucepan with a close-fitting lid is ideal for stovies. Peel eight or ten medium-sized potatoes (mealy for preference) and slice thickly. Peel three medium onions and slice thinly. Melt two tablespoonfuls of good beef dripping and fry the onions till lightly coloured. Add the potatoes, sprinkling them well with salt and pepper. Add about half a pint of water – no more – cover closely and cook very gently for an hour and a half, shaking the pan occasionally to prevent sticking. Serve alone, or as an accompaniment to cold meat. This is a grand supper dish on a cold night.

Skirlie or Skirl-in-the-Pan
Aberdeenshire and the North East

Oatmeal	onion
suet	salt, pepper

Chop two ounces of suet finely. Have a pan very hot and put in the suet. When it is melted, add one or two finely chopped onions and brown them well. Now add enough oatmeal to absorb the fat – a fairly thick mixture. Season to taste. Stir well until thoroughly cooked (a few minutes). Serve with potatoes.

From *The Scots Kitchen*
by F M McNeill, 1929

8 Eating out

Although Stuart Cranston created the original version, it was his sister Kate whose name became synonymous with the first Glasgow tearooms. With the help of her architect partner, Charles Rennie Mackintosh, who provided the avant garde interiors, she created a tearoom legend which in its day developed 'sight of the city' status on a par with the coffee houses of Vienna. Meanwhile her brother, who did not share her taste for modernity, carried on with his 'pure' tearooms, a commercial success but not so greatly celebrated.

Stuart Cranston was a tea merchant, with premises at 44 St Enoch Square, when an increased trade in tea and sugar imports was developing in Glasgow after the collapse of the tobacco trade. He followed the custom of the day of allowing clients to taste a

Kate Cranston, in about 1900, who gave her name to the famed Glasgow tearooms. She opened her first tearoom in 1878.

cup of tea before buying. The habit of 'perpendicular' lunchtime eating had developed for city businessmen and it was only a short step to introduce food, provide seats and serve tea instead of the traditional ale.

The consequences of poverty and urban deprivation had taken its toll in industrial cities like Glasgow, where alcoholism was a serious problem. Cranston and his sister belonged to the temperance movement, active in Glasgow at this time, and part of their incentive in developing the tearoom was to provide an alternative to the pub.

The first 'Cranston's Tearoom', opened by Stuart Cranston in 1875, was at the corner of Queen Street and Argyll Street (it was demolished in 1954). In 1878, Kate Cranston opened Miss Cranston's Crown Tearooms in 114 Argyle Street. With a distinctiveness described as 'Cranston from the chairs to the china', she went on in the same mode with another tearoom in Buchanan Street, and then in 1903 she created the highly sophisticated Miss Cranston's Willow Tearooms (now restored) in the more fashionable Sauchiehall Street.

By the turn of the century, tearooms had caught on, particularly with more progressive women who needed a place to meet outside the home which was not a pub. Though many of the old male order found the idea of the tearoom extremely distasteful, there were others who felt differently. The Bohemian élite of the city felt very much at home in the Cranston tearooms, partly because they could view their own paintings on the walls. And there was also the vast army of young city clerks, often with artistic temperaments, who felt at home in the Cranston atmosphere. She gave them tea, a place to smoke, talk, play cards or dominoes and, most importantly, she provided pretty waitresses with whom they could become friendly – even date.

In this first era of the Glasgow tearoom, the menus showed a versatile style of eating. First and foremost they satisfied a need for a simple cup of tea, but also provided a more substantial meal. From the 'Snack Teas' menu you could have: ham and egg;

sausage and bacon; a boiled country egg; a hot mutton pie; potted meat; kippered herring; or a fried split haddock. 'High Tea' was a fixed price affair. For 1s/3d there was a choice of ham and egg or filleted fish, three breads (varied) and a pot of tea. For 1s/6d you got an extra egg and chips with your fish.

If you wanted to go the whole hog, however, the 'A la Carte' high-tea menu included a choice of cold Tay salmon and salad, fried cod steak, Aberdeen haddock, baked fish custard, Wiltshire bacon and poached eggs, fried turkey egg, cold roast beef, lamb and tongue. Bread and butter or toast, scones and cakes, known as 'fancies', were accompanied by a pot of tea. While the tearooms publicized the high-tea tradition, distinguishing it from afternoon tea, everyday eating patterns of the working people were based around dinner, the main meal in the middle of the day, and tea, often a simple cold meal with bread and butter and perhaps cold meat accompanied by tea eaten in the early evening. The menu was directly related to the state of the families' finances.

While the Cranston tearooms survived for a while after World War I, and many other Cranston-type female characters such as Miss Buick and Miss Rombach carried on with the same style of tearoom, a number of family bakeries began to open tearooms. Craigs, Hubbards and Fullars were the leading bakers who brought to the tearoom an exceptionally high standard of baking. Craigs imported continental bakers and the 'French cake' was introduced to the city. Fullers were known for their éclairs and marzipan and walnut cake with toffee topping. Hubbards made 'paving stones' which were square-shaped chewy crisp gingerbreads with a hard icing on top. Craigs, the most successful and popular of the bakery chains, were also renowned for their chocolate liqueur cakes.

Because the 'spend' in the old tearooms was frequently very low, their economic success depended to a large extent on cheap female labour, which after World War II became less available. By the 1950s social habits were also changing. Starched tablecloths and good furniture may have satisfied the previous generation, but young people in the post-war years were looking for something more modern. Old bakery firms were taken over by conglomerates and only a few bakery tea-rooms have survived to the present day.

From the late nineteenth century, however, and throughout the twentieth, a number of different immigrant communities have settled in Scotland, introducing new eating styles. Among them, the most important and influential have been those who extended their food culture into ethnic restaurants. Since the 1950s Italian, Chinese and Indo-Pakistani restaurants have been a major influence in widening the people's food experience.

The Italians were the first; fleeing poverty at home in late nine-teenth-century Italy, they had begun by selling ice cream and fried chips (see Chapter 6). But besides the ice-cream parlours and fish-and-chip restaurants which subsequently developed, they also extended their influence to Italian restaurants and well-stocked delicatessens. In the delis they sold authentic Italian produce, often imported from Italy, or made on the premises using family recipes for breads, pizzas, sausages, cooked meats and pastas, creating a loyalty not only among the Scots-Italian community but also among the native Scots.

Though the delis originally served the large homesick Italian community with basic home-made pasta and native olive oil – unobtainable in Scotland – they gradually developed into highly sophisticated emporiums of Italian produce. Some are on their way to becoming legends, such as Valvona and Crolla in Edinburgh and Fratelli Sarti in Glasgow.

While the Italians were able to influence the native Scots through both the restaurant and the deli, the main influence of the Indian and Pakistani communities has been through the restaurant. Those who settled in Scotland after Indian indepen-dence in 1947 had a strong influence on eating habits, particularly in the urban areas where they mainly settled, bringing with them, first and foremost, the subtleties of spices and an imaginative cooking style. Though their early restaurant exploits were often

Italian café in Broughton Street, Edinburgh, 1907. The café was opened by the Pacitti family from Naples. SEA

based on what they perceived the Scots expected of a 'hot' curry dish, their style has been modified over the years. Still often 'hot' and spicy, there is now a more sensitive approach to the natural flavours of the raw materials. The 1980s saw the development of a number of restaurants where much more emphasis was placed on delicate spicing and less on chilli-hot mouth-burners.

Though the first Chinese restaurant in Britain was opened in Piccadilly Circus in 1908, it was not until after World War II that demand for Chinese food really took off. A liking for oriental food had been developed during the war, by British forces serving in the East, and when Mao's regime was officially recognized by the British in 1951, large numbers of Chinese fled the country or were stranded in Britain. The cooks started opening restaurants, and noodles and rice became an important part of the eating-out scene.

Another aspect of Chinese cooking, which had an important influence, was 'chow' (stir-frying). It was in the kitchens of Buddhist temples and monasteries that vegetarian cookery was most highly developed. A small amount of oil heated in a wok was used to cook, firstly the strong-flavoured garlic, ginger and onions, followed by finely chopped vegetables. It became the basis for Chinese restaurant menus as the popularity of oriental eating-out continued to grow.

One of the most successful and influential foreigners was the Greek Cypriot Reo Stakis who arrived in Glasgow selling lace from a motorbike and eventually earned enough money to buy the old Ceylon Tearoom at the top of St Vincent Street. He turned it into the Prince's Restaurant in 1949 and began the systematic takeover of the old-fashioned tearooms, turning them into modern restaurants providing a congenial atmosphere and affordable food which had been the Kate Cranston formula less than half a century earlier. A traditional Stakis menu might begin with a prawn cocktail, followed by steak-and-chips, and end with a black forest gâteau, accompanied by a bottle of cheap and cheerful 'plonk'.

9 A natural food producer

Since the end of World War II, Scotland has been increasing its primary food production at a greater rate than domestic consumption. So while the country is becoming more self-sufficient, there is also more available for export. Because of the large areas of unpolluted waters around the coastline, fish and shellfish have become a major export, with new developments in commercial aquaculture of shellfish and salmon. Animal breeding is mainly of cattle and sheep rather than pigs and poultry. In the dairying areas large-scale cheddar-making accounts for most of the cheese production, though there are also a number of flourishing small specialist artisan cheesemakers. Some have developed new cheese types while others have revived some of the traditional cheeses such as crowdie, caboc and Dunlop cheese.

On the whole, the emphasis of grain production is on barley and oats rather than wheat. Vegetables grown in largest quanti-

Home-made Orkney cheeses made by Mrs Pirie at Orphir in Orkney, 1961. Alexander Fenton, SEA

ties are potatoes and turnips rather than salad vegetables. Recently, commercial growing of broccoli has become a major Scottish export and the traditional tomato growing in the Clyde Valley has been revived, while commercial fruit production concentrates on soft fruits rather than apples and pears.

The long hours of summer light, which Scotland shares with other northern European countries, combined with a cool, damp ripening season, have made soft berries a common part of the summer diet. The climate and soils of Angus and Tayside (also the Clyde valley) have provided the best conditions for a commercial soft-fruit-growing industry which now produces around 90% of the British raspberry crop as well as other commercial crops of strawberries, tayberries, blackcurrants, redcurrants, gooseberries, and more recently, high bush blueberries.

Wild berry-picking is largely confined to brambles, wild raspberries, rowans and sloes, though blaeberries also grow in profusion

A young raspberry picker in 1960. Intensive seasonal labour is required to gather the soft fruit crops. SEA

on the Scottish hills. The market in wild berries (as also the market in wild mushrooms) has never been exploited in the same way as other northern Europeans, such as the Scandinavians, have maintained an interest in their wild cloudberries and arctic brambles.

Native cattle in the Highlands were an important part of the clan-based economy until the early nineteenth century. Used as a supply of milk, cheese and butter, the dairy cows were driven during the summer months to the hill pastures and the women and children moved with them to live in 'shielings' (dwellings in the hills). While the women made cheese and butter, the men herded the surplus cattle south, along ancient drove roads, to Lowland markets where they were bought for 'finishing' on more lush Lowland pastures.

By the mid-nineteenth century the trade had declined, partly as a result of the break-up of the clan system followed by the Highland Clearances, but also because of a demand for better quality beef. The Highland cattle which were driven along the ancient drove roads were often four to five years old, and their carcasses did not provide the kind of tender meat which could be obtained from young animals, reared and fattened on the new fodder crops near to the market.

Although it suffered in popularity, the breed was encouraged by certain lairds, notably the Stewart brothers of Harris, MacNeil of Barra, the Duke of Hamilton and the Duke of Argyll. Stock seems to have been selected from island and mainland populations with no evidence of Lowland blood having been brought in. Hardiness has remained a key characteristic of the breed. Like the Aberdeen Angus, it is quite closely related to the Galloway with a common ancestry in primitive native stock, but influenced in its physical development by the more rugged and more severe weather conditions of the Highlands.

The breed society was founded in 1884 with 516 bulls listed in the first herd book, most of which were black or dun. Some went to Canada in 1882 and in the 1920s exports were made to the USA and South America. Today there has been a revival of interest in the breed, particularly for the quality of its meat. Butchers who have taken to specializing in pure Highland beef have attracted a loyal, and growing, following from both the domestic and catering market.

Though the most widely known Scottish breed is the Aberdeen Angus, it is also the most recently established. Pioneer breeder, Hugh Watson (1780-1865) from Keillor near Dundee, first showed his black polled cattle in 1820, and by 1829 was sending some of his stock from the Highland Show in Perth to Smithfield. The trade to London of prime beef in carcass (sending only the most expensive cuts) developed, alongside the success of Watson's herd. This new, and more sophisticated, method became the norm with the completion of the railway line to London in 1850.

Watson is regarded as having 'fixed' the type of the new breed and by the time his herd was dispersed, in 1861, it had been highly selected within itself. For the fifty years of its existence, it seems that he never bought in a bull. He sold stock to William McCombie (1805-1880) of Tillyfour, near Aberdeen, who carried on with the breeding, attaching the same importance to meeting the requirements of the London trade. The breed's main rival in Scotland was Amos Cruickshank's Scotch Shorthorn (established in the 1830s when he and his brother became tenants of an Aberdeenshire farm) which could be fattened more rapidly, but which did not milk so well and was less hardy. To overcome

An Arbroath butcher's shop in about 1915. The small boy in the doorway took over the business at the age of 15, on his father's death. SEA

its problems, and introduce more rapid fattening in the Aberdeen Angus, the characteristics of the two breeds were combined by crossing them and the Aberdeen-Angus cross Shorthorn became the source of most of the prime beef produced in Scotland.

Changes have occurred in the breed in the last three decades. Firstly a peak demand developed in the 1960s for a small, thick bull with a lot of meat, a trend which was reversed with entry to the European Union when a fashion developed in the 1970s and 80s for a taller, leaner animal with a minimum of fat. But the meat did not have the succulence and flavour required by the modern consumer. Thus the aim now is to have meat that has a marbling of fat through it, to give a healthy product that is succulent and tasty. This approach has stimulated a new era in the history of the breed as retailers are now establishing more effectively the importance of the Aberdeen Angus tag for its fine flavour and succulence. Increasingly, they are demonstrating the breed's quality (in contrast to quantity) by joining the certification scheme which allows them to market the meat as Aberdeen-Angus.

Salmon has always featured importantly in the Scottish diet. Early salmon fisheries on the rivers, Tay, Spey, Tweed, Don and Dee produced large catches which were eaten fresh in summer and 'kippered' (smoked and dried) in winter. The quantity caught each year was such that it was an everyday food of the people and became so firmly fixed in the minds of the upper classes in Scotland as a cheap working man's food that a Highland gentleman, on visiting London, made the mistake of choosing the beef for himself and the salmon for his servant. 'The Cook, who attended him humoured the jest, and the Master's eating was Eight Pence and Duncan's came to almost as many Shillings.' (Burt, *Letters from the North of Scotland*, 1730)

While supplies of wild salmon remained plentiful for the best part of the nineteenth century there has been a gradual, but serious, decline this century. Over-fishing and netting have been just two of the problems and research is currently taking place to discover the reasons.

Salmon farming began on the west coast in 1969 and has spread to islands, particularly the islands of Shetland where they market their salmon separately from the rest of Scotland. It has created many problems, both environmental and commercial, but aquaculture has brought an important occupation to a remote and otherwise declining population, whose traditions have always been based on harvesting from the sea. Many of the problems have been solved with research and experimentation so that the farming can be more efficient and less environmentally damaging. Skilled farming can produce a high-quality fish with an important potential. Already it has made its name in the markets of Europe gaining a French *Label Rouge* accolade of prime quality. Currently Scotland has around 97 smokehouses smoking about 14,000 tons of fish from Scottish waters in a year. The relationship which has been built up between farmer and smoker is one of the best guarantees for the future success of an ancient and distinguished smoking industry.

Preservation of salmon in Scotland began with a method known as 'kippering' which can be traced back to records of a monastery in Fife (dated 1479), when the local salmon fishery was obliged to deliver three dozen salmon a year, either 'fresh or kippered'. The salmon sent for kippering had spawned, described as 'spent', lacking fat and moisture and therefore easier to pickle and smoke. The Dutch *kuppen* meaning 'to spawn' was applied originally to a spent fish but was also applied to a spent salmon which had been cured. Kippered salmon is mentioned in the household book of James V (1513-1542). From an expedient way of dealing with less than prime fish, curers have – over several centuries – changed the old kippered salmon into one of Scotland's most prestigious gourmet foods.

While the clan system survived, native game formed a large part of the diet shared out among people. As the natural resources of red deer (venison), grouse, ptarmigan, wild duck and goose, capercaillie and hare were gradually taken over by shooting estates, game became a rarity in the everyday diet of the people. Confined to poaching-for-the-pot, the people, however, continued to make use of it clandestinely, and cooking traditions have survived, handed down through the generations. Native Highlanders do not make the mistake of meddling with its natural character by adding too many miscellaneous flavours; a brace of mountain grouse (ptarmigan) might be roasting in the oven, a pot of mountain hare broth on the stove, a fry-up of venison liver and bacon for breakfast. They understand how to contrast the rich deep flavours: blending them in a slow-cooked soup-cum-stew with vegetables and serving with the native floury Golden Wonder potatoes.

In recent years more shooting estates have sought to market their game through consortia and the availablity in Scotland has increased. Post-World War II, about 90% of the best Scottish wild venison was exported to Germany, but this market is changing as Scots gradually discover the advantages of the lean, non-intensively reared, well-flavoured meat.

A successful week's stalking. Today, venison production is on a commercial scale and there are significant exports of this traditional Scottish food. SEA

10 Traditional baking

It has been remarked that if every Frenchwoman is born with a wooden spoon in her hand, then every Scotswoman has a rolling pin under her arm. The Scots skill with a rolling pin is almost certainly due to the ancient peasant tradition of rolling out a thick paste of meal and cooking it on hot stone or iron plate. In its original form it was most commonly made into a hard 'cake', often with a mix of barley and oat flours, which was eaten as the daily bread of the people.

When Burns referred to Scotland as the 'land o' cakes', he did not mean the sweetened oven-baked variety, which have now become associated with the word, but the hard 'cake' baked on a hot stone or girdle. The word 'cake' originally referred to flat unleavened items which were baked hard on both sides. 'A cake of bread', meaning something baked hard, was the origin of what eventually became known as the 'oatcake'. The association with oats developed when it finally became the staple grain, gradually

Clark's bakery in Dundee, 1973, with traditional scones and pancakes. SEA

taking over from barley which was subsequently used mostly for making whisky.

In Scots girdle-baking parlance, any large round item baked on the girdle is known as a 'bannock'. When the bannock is cut into quarters, each quarter is known as a 'farl'. The integration of hard oatcakes into eating habits was such that they became symbolic food, used to record events and taking different forms and shapes. A 'crying' oatcake was made with cream and sugar when a baby was born. An oaten 'mill bannock' was made to celebrate the harvest home. At Halloween, very salty oatcakes were made which were

Oatmeal bannocks being prepared by Marianne Calder in Dunnet, Caithness, 1969. SEA

thought to induce dreams. 'Teethin bannocks' were made with butter and oatmeal for babies to cut teeth on. And oat farls with a slice of cheese on top were given to children who came round the doors looking for a treat at Hogmanay.

When Highland women took their children along with the croft animals to the hill shielings in summer, they also made primitive oatcakes on stones heated by the peat fire. Since wheat was not grown in the Highlands, it is unlikely that this Highland oatcake would have had any wheaten flour with a gluten content which would have helped to hold it together. Pressed out by hand, it was their thickness which ensured their stability, though recipes also added an egg and hot milk making a thicker heavier oatcake. In contrast to the thinner Lowland variety, it was a sustaining oatcake, used as hard tack for hunting men.

Very thin brittle oatcakes, made into quarters (farls) which curl at the edges as they dry out, are a more sophisticated version. Used as a vehicle for other things, this type of oatcake has become linked with breakfast marmalade and honey, or as an accompanying biscuit with tangy cheeses.

While hard unleavened cakes were the first girdle-baked bread, the advent of commercial raising agents in the late nineteenth century introduced new girdle traditions. Large round bannocks were made thicker and lighter (see beremeal bannock, page 45) and the flavoured scone developed, sometimes as a farl, sometimes shaped with a round cutter. Only two items of girdle baking, the oatcake and the potato scone, preserve the original unleavened form, both made first into a bannock shape and then cut into farls.

Scots pancakes are another girdle-baking development, made from a flour, raising agent, egg and milk batter and distinct from the French crêpe, known in England as a pancake. The Scots pancake is small, round, soft and spongy, and about half an inch thick; it is sometimes known as a 'dropped scone'. A Scots crumpet, on the other hand, is made from the same batter mix, but the consistency is runnier, spreading to around six inches in diameter on the girdle and with a thickness of about a quarter of an inch.

Described by the Scottish Association of Master Bakers, not as a common biscuit, but as a 'speciality item of flour confectionery', shortbread is today one of the most commercially successful Scottish bakery items, exported in decorative Scottish tins by the million around the world. The original version of shortbread was made by adding melted butter to an everyday bread dough, making it something more akin to a butterized version of an English lardy cake. The result should probably have been described as a 'short cake' or 'buttery cake'.

Old festive shortbreads made by the rural communities were shaped into large round bannocks or rectangles, not cut neatly into squares or wedges, but broken up into uneven chunks, the pieces piled high on an old ashet. Recipes today have now totally abandoned the yeast leavening, but two of the old festive bannocks survive in the Pitcaithly Bannock with nuts, caraway and preserved lemon and orange peel and in the Yetholm Bannock with crystallized ginger.

Around the early nineteenth century, the more genteel 'petti-coat tails' appeared on elegant afternoon tea stands, though there was some confusion about the origin of the name. Was it another Scottish borrowing from the French – a corruption of *petites gatelles*, – or was it a simple analogy with the shape of bell-hoop petticoats once worn by court ladies?

Though Black Bun is inextricably linked with the Scots and Hogmanay, not all Scots regard it as an essential element of the festivities. It has no real following in the Highlands or in the North-east of Scotland where it has never been part of their winter solstice celebrations. Their spiced and fruited speciality is a clootie dumpling and not the richer more sophisticated bakery item more akin to a Christmas pudding in a pie crust.

The bakers of Edinburgh, according to 'Meg Dods' (1826), exported buns in sizes – '4, 8, 10, 12, 16 and more pounds' from

A North Uist kitchen with evidence of baking equipment on shelves and table. J R Baldwin, SEA

Edinburgh to England, Ireland and Wales. At this stage the bun had lost its original name of Plum Cake, and had been rechristened a 'Scotch Christmas Bun' though Meg Dods still makes it according to the earliest plum cake recipes using a yeast dough, spiced, fruited and enclosed in a casing of plain bread dough.

Strictly speaking, an enriched mound of bread dough in Scotland should have been called a bannock, as in the Selkirk Bannock, not a 'bun'. Why this became known as a 'bun' may have had something to do with the fact that it was exported in large quantities, a 'bun' being more readily understood outside Scotland than the native 'bannock'. At any rate it seems clear that enterprising bakers in Lowland Scotland around the turn of the nineteenth century discovered the value of a richly spiced, fruity cake wrapped in a protective outer covering.

The recipe on the left, first published in Mrs McLintock's, *Receipts for Cookery and Pastry-Work* 1736, the first published cookery book in Scotland, may have been their inspiration.

Scotland has a fascinating range of regional baking specialities, each with their own story. Fed up with living off hard ship's biscuit on long trips to the North Sea, the Aberdeen fisherman persuaded their friendly local bakers to make something with taste which would keep for a fortnight. The baker started his experiments, cutting off a lump from his daily batch of bread dough. Knowing that if he put

---

Plum Cake

Take a Peck of Flour, two Pound of Butter; rub the Butter among the Flour, till it be like Flour again; take 12 Eggs, a lb of Sugar, beat them well together; then take a Mutchkin of sweet Barm, half a Mutchkin of Brandy, then your Flour with the beaten Eggs and Sugar, and put in the Barm and Brandy and work all well together; then take ten lb of Currans, 2 lb Cordecidron [lemon peel], 2 lb of Orange-peel, 2lb blanched Almonds cut, half an Ounce of Cinnamon, half an Ounce of Nutmeg and Cloves, half an Ounce of Carvey-seed [caraway]; take off the fourth Part of the Leaven for a Cover, and work the Fruits and Spices among the rest, then put on the Cover, and send it to the Oven.

some meat dripping from the butcher into the dough it would make it keep better, he rolled out the dough, covered it with fat, folded it, rolled it, kneaded, and then cut it up into misshapen mounds which he flattened into the same large thin round shape as his normal softies (rolls). These were 'butterie rowies'. His fisherman friend was delighted. And so, too, were the people of the town who sampled the new ship's biscuit. The news of the crisp, crunchy rowie (roll), with its faintly burnt saltiness, spread, and it was soon being made by every baker on the east coast, its practical, homely shape and satisfying taste endearing it to the community.

It has none of the stylish pretensions of a French croissant, though its ingredients are roughly the same. Thanks to the loyalty of the north-east people, it has survived such competition as the industrialization of a baking industry which has seen the end of other time-consuming products, like rowies, made by hand. Shape, size, thickness, taste, texture and price all vary around the Aberdeenshire area, though there is fairly general agreement that too much sogginess, doughiness or breadiness does not belong in a proper Aberdeen rowie. The much softer 'bready' rowie made in Dundee, is disparagingly described by Aberdonians as a 'collapsed softie'.

The Dundee Cake has a world reputation. City legend has it that it originated as a by-product of the Keiller marmalade industry, though by the early twentieth century it had been widely copied throughout the UK. In the 1980s, Keillers was taken over by a multi-national company and the gentleman's agreement which had existed in the city that only Keillers made the cake was abandoned. Now other bakers in the city have joined bakers around Britain, who never had any moral inhibitions about making it.

The Keiller cake was a rich buttery sultana cake with no other fruits, no spices, no flavouring essences and no cherries. The flavourings were the orange peel and almonds which came from Spain. Bakers in the city who now make the cake point out it is not enough to put a covering of almonds on an everyday fruit cake. The Dundee Cake is a special-occasion cake with high quality ingredients and an expensive covering of whole, not flaked, blanched almonds.

It was a baker in Selkirk, Robbie Douglas, who opened a shop in the Market Place in 1859 and drew attention to the quality of his rich yeasted bannocks, creating such a reputation that in time the bannock took the name of Selkirk. His bannock depended, he claimed, on the quality of the butter, and he insisted on using the best butter from cows grazing on neighbouring pastures. He used only the best sultanas from Turkey, and together with his baking skills produced the legendary round, bun-shaped bannock. It is recorded that on her visit to Sir Walter Scott's granddaughter at Abbotsford in 1867 Queen Victoria refused all else on the sumptuous tea spread, save a a slice of the Douglas bannock.

While a number of bakers now make the bannock, the original Douglas recipe is said to have been handed on from Alex Dalgetty, one of the bakers who worked with Douglas. Dalgetty's descendants continue to make the 'original' at their bakery in Galashiels, though Houstons in Hawick now own the bakery where Douglas made the original bannock. Hossacks in Kelso have recently developed the Tweed Bannock using wholemeal flour.

Originally made with a portion of everyday bread dough, the genuine bannock-bakers make up a special bannock dough. Some, but not all, continue to follow the original method of a 'sponge' dough with a long overnight slow fermentation producing a finer flavour.

Forfar has lent its name to another distinctive bakery item. Though a 'bridie', in other parts of the country, has become the generic name for a crescent-shaped puff-pastry turnover with a filling of common sausagemeat, the original Forfar bridie is flatter, larger, and more like the shape of a horse's hoof than a true crescent. The layer of meat spreads out to the edge of the pastry, so that for every bite there is a mouthful of steak filling.

Bakers in Forfar have been making the bridie for over a hundred years. The earliest bridie baker is reputed to be Jollys, no longer in existence, but where they were sold around the turn of the century hot from the oven as a market-day treat to the farm hands who gathered in the town on Saturdays. The bridie's origins are disputed between a number of claims, one of which is the much-quoted story relating to Margaret Bridie of Glamis, who became renowned for her meat pastries, which she sold in the Buttermarket in Forfar. Another theory is based on a claim by one baker whose family business goes back four generations to the earliest bridies, that because meat was eaten rarely by the people, and usually only as a treat, on special occasions such as weddings, christenings and funerals, it was made for the bride's meal, the baker making a special lucky horseshoe-shaped pastry with meat inside. Forfar bakers report that they are still made for weddings, as well as other celebrations, but like fish and chips in a poke, they have become part of a more informal hand-to-mouth eating which loses its attraction when plates and cutlery intervene.

11 The cooking renaissance

In cookery, as in all the arts, there are periods of ebb and flow, not just in the day-to-day basic foods of the people cooking at a fairly simple level, but also in the higher echelons of gastronomy. In both fields there have been some remarkable changes throughout the twentieth century.

A strict Calvinist morality is sometimes given as an excuse for the lack of gastronomic appreciation found, not just in Scotland but throughout the United Kingdom, in the latter half of the twentieth century. In England the Puritans and Oliver Cromwell put an end to feasting, while in Scotland it was the Protestant church and John Knox who regarded good eating and drinking as sinful gluttony. Yet the idea that this has been solely responsible for the very different approach to eating and drinking which has developed in Britain, in comparison with France or Italy, is misleading.

Scotland, in particular, can be classed along with the other cold countries of Northern Europe who have been deprived of the warm climate more conducive to a relaxed style of eating and drinking. A

A cast-iron range was a prized feature of kitchens until well into the twentieth century. SEA

way of eating has developed which has been more appropriate to a long cold winter. A traditional cooking style has been created based on warming broths, sustaining stews and filling puddings.

Throughout the twentieth century, Scotland has also been greatly involved, along with the rest of Britain, in fighting wars. Inevitably this created a form of siege-mentality, totally alien to the relaxed appreciation of the pleasures of the table. Those who lived through the war years were obliged to scrimp and save, and do without. Food was fodder, not fun. And even when the wars were over, many continued to discourage their children from 'wasting' money on food. Rationing lasted in Britain for thirteen years, which was longer than in any other European country, and inevitably some of this attitude has lingered on, often in an

Plucking chickens for an Eriskay wedding, 1960. The chickens were then cooked in a washing-boiler. Kenneth Robertson, Stornoway, SEA

involuntary, unconscious way. But because it became an ingrained habit for at least two generations of the twentieth century, it has not been so easy to change the flow.

The most remarkable change which has taken place in the twentieth century, and the one which has the potential to make the most significant change in eating habits in the future, has been the development of the modern food-processing and food-retailing industries, more sophisticated and much larger in Britain than in any other European country. Take away the technology of the last fifty years and life becomes a tad difficult. Freezerless and microwaveless, attempting to cook from scratch means a lot more time and energy spent buying and preparing food. The art of cookery is at the crossroads between tradition and technology.

Either traditional cooking skills are abandoned, or they are preserved in some form which makes practical sense. The difficulty of preserving them has been influenced by the fact that many more women today return to paid work outside the home within a few years of childbirth, yet continue to feed, clothe and comfort their children. It has created remarkable opportunities for the food industry. The low participation of men in domestic work has also contributed to the rise of the microwave and the cook-chill meal. If this continues, then technological cooking seems set for a bright future. As parents cease to turn basic ingredients into meals, and as cooking skills drop out of school curricula, a new generation will emerge without the basic food knowledge and cooking skills needed to be able to use fresh, unprocessed foods and turn them into meals. The consequences of lost cooking skills, and lack of food knowledge, is a concern found in varying degrees, not just in Scotland, but throughout the world.

Though technology might look as though it is set to take over the cooking arts and influence the eating habits of the future, another movement is also working in the opposite direction. It began in the 1950s, not in Scotland, but with the pioneering English food writer Elizabeth David, who injected some of the relaxed rhythm of Mediterranean food philosophy into the British diet. About the same time, the political commentator Raymond Postgate had become so incensed by the gastronomic poverty of the post-war restaurant that he decided to launch a club of like-minded members. They filed reports about their eating-out experiences, and *The Good Food Guide* was born.

Pre-war, sophisticated eating places had been grand hotels, but now a band of educated amateurs joined the classically trained professional chefs, in attempting to wrench the country's appreciation of food out of its depression and into something which could match the gastronomy of other more enlightened countries of Europe.

Thanks to the liberating effect of the 'nouvelle' movement in the 1970s and 80s, restaurant menus changed. Now led by the availability of the best-quality local raw materials rather than a fixed range of dishes dictated by the French repertoire of classical dishes, gastronomy moved into the platescape and pretentious-ness era of *nouvelle cuisine*. It may have created a storm, but it broke the slavish British addiction to 'haute' cuisine as the disad-vantages of rich saucery and complicated, time-consuming and expensive cooking procedures masked the natural tastes of good quality raw materials.

As the economic recession of the 1980s took a grip, the use of native seafood, game, beef, lamb and soft fruits became a more important feature on restaurant and hotel menus. No longer embarrassed about their ancestry, native cooks began to establish an original and innovative style which gradually gained in popu-larity. It now combines more honestly the things regarded as appropriate to its heritage. Special Scottish foods, made, caught or grown by dedicated producers, fishermen and farmers are playing a more important role. Recently, those involved in the Scottish cooking renaissance have felt self-confident enough to include on their menus modernized versions of old peasant-style dishes such as skirlie, stovies and clapshot. A team of Scottish chefs cooking recently at a UK food promotion in the Waldorf Astoria in New York gave the guests a roast leg of Scottish lamb stuffed with a black pudding made by a Stornoway butcher.

This is not to say that enlightened cooks in the modern kitchen have not been inspired also by other cuisines. While in the past the most prestigious cachet was always French, now menus reflect a more eclectic approach, integrating some elements of Oriental and Mediterranean cooking styles which are appropriate to the climate and eating habits of the Scots.

Many of these innovations have resulted from a direct contact with immigrants who have settled in the country, others have developed through travel abroad. But whatever the influence, they illustrate the historic Scottish tradition of looking outwards, gathering from other cultures what is appropriate, while retaining a strong sense of Scottish character.

Boys boiling potatoes on the street, and clearly also trying to keep warm. Potatoes became a staple Scottish food in the late eighteenth century. Walter Geikie

FURTHER READING

Historical cookery books

BROWN, Martha Unpublished manuscript recipes dated 1710, private collection in Ayr and Cunningham Public Library

CLARK, Lady of Tillypronie *The Cookery Book of Lady Clark of Tillypronie* edited by Catherine Frere, 1909, Lewes 1994

CLELAND, E *A New and Easy Method of Cookery*, Edinburgh 1755

DALGAIRNS, Mrs *Practice of Cookery*, Edinburgh 1829

DODS, Mistress Margaret (Meg) *The Cook and Housewife's Manual*, Edinburgh 1826 facsimile, London 1988

FRAZER, Mrs *The Practice of cookery, pastry, pickling, preserving*, Edinburgh 1791

MCLINTOCK, Mrs *Receipts for Cookery and Pastry-Work, 1736*. The first published cookery book in Scotland. Facsimile, Aberdeen 1986

MCNEILL, F M *The Scots Kitchen*, Glasgow 1929

WENTWORTH, Josie A *Janie Ellice's Recipes 1846-1859*, London 1974

WHYTE, Hamish (ed) *Lady Castlehill's Cook Book*, Glasgow 1976 (from manuscript recipes by Martha Lockhart, The Lady Castlehill, 1712, collection in Mitchell Library, Glasgow.)

Other cookery books and general books

BROWN, C *Scottish Regional Recipes*, 3rd reprint Edinburgh 1992

BROWN, C *Scottish Cookery*, 4th reprint Edinburgh 1995

BROWN, C *Broths to Bannocks*, London 1990

FENTON, A *Scottish Country Life*, Edinburgh 1987

FITZGIBBON, T *A Taste of Scotland*, London 1970

FOULIS, J *Foulis of Ravelston's Account book: 1671-1707*, Edinburgh 1894

GIBSON, A J S and SMOUT, T C *Prices, Food and Wages in Scotland 1550-1780*, Cambridge 1995

HOPE, A *A Caledonian Feast*, Edinburgh 1986

MARTIN, M *A Description of the Western Islands of Scotland*, Edinburgh 1703

MACDOUGALL, J *Highland Postbag, the Correspondence of Four MacDougall Chiefs 1715-1865*, London 1984

TANNAHILL, R *Food in History*, St Albans 1975

WILSON, C A *Food and Drink in Britain*, London 1973

WILSON, J *Noctes Ambrosianae*, 4 vols, Edinburgh 1855

PLACES TO VISIT

Many small museums throughout Scotland contain material related to food and its preparation, and castles and country houses often include kitchens. Here is a selection.

Aberfeldy, Perthshire: *The Aberfeldy Mill* (oatmeal).

Alford, Aberdeenshire: *Montgarrie Mills* (oatmeal).

Anstruther, Fife: *Scottish Fisheries Museum*.

Arbroath Museum, Angus: *Arbroath Museum* (smokies).

Arnol, Isle of Lewis: *The Black House*.

Auchendrain, Inveraray: *reconstructed farming township*.

Blair Atholl, Perthshire: *Blair Atholl Mill* (oatmeal).

Cupar, Fife: *Hill of Tar t Mansion House*, National Trust for Scotland (Edwardian kitchen).

Edinburgh: *The Georgian House*, National Trust for Scotland (kitchen).

Edinburgh: the *Museum of Scotland*, due to open in 1998, will include displays linked with food and drink, from prehistory to the present.

Edinburgh: *Scottish Agricultural Museum*, Ingliston (country life)

Ellon, Aberdeenshire: *Pitmedden Garden and Museum of Farming Life*.

Fort William, Inverness-shire: *The West Highland Museum*.

Glamis, Angus: *Angus Folk Museum*, National Trust for Scotland.

Glasgow: *The Tenement House*, National Trust for Scotland (kitchen).

Golspie, Sutherland: *Dunrobin Castle*.

Golspie, Sutherland: *The Golspie Mill* (beremeal/peasemeal).

Kingussie, Inverness-shire: *Highland Folk Museum*.

Kilmuir, Skye: *Skye Museum of Island Life*.

Lauder, Berwickshire: *Thirlestane Castle* (kitchens).

Moniaive, Dumfriesshire: *Maxwelton Museum* (kitchen, dairy and farming material).

Newton Stewart, Wigtownshire: *The Museum* (kitchen utensils).

Selkirk: *Bowhill* (Victorian kitchen).

Stirling: *Castle* (reconstructed kitchens)